Nabendu Ghosh (1917-2007) was a dancer, novelist, short-story writer, film director, actor and screenwriter. His oeuvre of work includes thirty novels and fifteen collections of short stories, including *That Bird Called Happiness: Stories*, edited by Ratnottama Sengupta (Speaking Tiger, 2018). As scriptwriter, he penned cinematic classics such as *Devdas, Bandini, Sujata, Parineeta, Majhli Didi* and *Abhimaan*. And, as part of a team of iconic film directors and actors, he was instrumental in shaping an entire age of Indian cinema. He was the recipient of numerous literary and film awards, including the Bankim Puraskar, the Bibhuti Bhushan Sahitya Arghya, the Filmfare Best Screenplay Award and the National Film Award for Best First Film of a Director.

Ratnottama Sengupta, formerly Arts Editor of *The Times of India*, teaches mass communication and film appreciation, curates film festivals and art exhibitions, and writes books. The daughter of Nabendu Ghosh, she has written *Krishna's Cosmos*, a biography of the pioneering printmaker Krishna Reddy, and also entries on Hindi films for *Encyclopedia Britannica*. She has been a member of the Central Board of Film Certification, served on the jury of the National Film Awards, and has herself won a National Film Award. In 2017, she directed *And They Made Classics*, a documentary about Nabendu Ghosh. And in 2018, she edited Nabendu Ghosh's book of short stories, *That Bird Called Happiness* (Speaking Tiger).

PRAISE FOR NABENDU GHOSH

'Through the 1940s, your writings reflected your progressive thought that confronted the brutality of imperialist activities. Your world of letters brought home to Bengali readers your pain, your anger, your desire to free Mother India of her chains. With the mind-set of a historian, you portrayed the ugly face of communalism unleashed by Independence. It revealed to the populace the many walls that fragmented our land. A worshipper of humanity, you waged relentless battles against this compartmentalization of our identities in the name of caste, creed, colour and class. Love for Man is your signature tune.' —Citation from the Bangiya Sahitya Parishad Award

'As a writer and as a creative individual, Nabendu Ghosh has never believed evil is man's natural state. Along with his characters, he has been confronting it, as always, fighting and surviving on tension and hope.' —Mrinal Sen

'His devotion to Bengali literature and his creativity in the language is a matter of great joy...' —Sunil Gangopadhyay

'Nabendu Ghosh's perfect characterisation enabled any director to shoot the film with ease. He had the rare ability to pen the pulse of a character. His scripts brought to films a literary value that was missing...' —Dilip Kumar, *The Statesman*

'It is not easy to stay behind the silver screen and touch people's hearts through the screen. Legendary screenwriter Nabendu Ghosh has succeeded in doing this effortlessly. I have had the privilege of seeing the magic of his scripting in *Devdas, Sujata, Teesri Kasam, Bandini* and *Parineeta*... I am delighted that a translation of his stories is ready for the reading public outside Bengal.' —Gopalkrishna Gandhi

'Nabendu Ghosh is a writer I have always loved. He was not only one of our finest Bengali authors but his screenplays defined the best of Hindi cinema. Films like *Devdas, Sujata, Teesri Kasam, Bandini* and the very memorable *Abhimaan* still stay alive in our hearts because of his amazing narrative skills. He will be remembered as long as Hindi cinema lives.' —Pritish Nandy

'I was astonished to learn that the original story of *Kaagaz Ke Phool* was written by Nabendu Ghosh... *Teesri Kasam* also showed his genius...as did *Sujata* and *Bandini*...' —Waheeda Rehman, Anandalok

'There was a time when most screenwriters came from literature and, so, respected literature. This essentially meant that the screenwriter keeps the essence of a literary work intact while taking cinematic liberties with it. Nabendu-da was the epitome of this. On the other hand, his short stories were cinematic and didn't leave their focus on the visual quality and emotions. He was a man of cinema in literature, and man of literature in cinema.' —Nitish Bharadwaj

Mistress of Melodies

Stories of Courtesans and Prostituted Women

Nabendu Ghosh

Edited by Ratnottama Sengupta

Foreword by Muzaffar Ali

SPEAKING TIGER

SPEAKING TIGER BOOKS LLP
4381/4, Ansari Road, Daryaganj
New Delhi 110002

Published in paperback by Speaking Tiger Books 2020

ISBN: 978-81-944908-6-9
eISBN: 978-81-944908-7-6

10 9 8 7 6 5 4 3 2 1

Typeset in Adobe Caslon Pro by SÜRYA, New Delhi
Printed at Sanat Printers, Kundli

Contents

Foreword

Zone of Purity in the River of Flesh

Nabendu Ghosh takes you deep into an emotion that has been the pride of the cinema of Bengal, the cinema of realism and the romance of culture.

In *Mistress of Melodies* the author traverses the streets of that dynamic, ever-changing city—Calcutta. Streets that have heard the hoof-beats of horses and resounded with the clanging music of crowded trams. From the luxuriant art of the sarangi to the thhaap of the tabla; from the gentle sur of the mellifluous singer to the wilderness of unrequited love and unfulfilled passion—he measures them all in the currency of an era now lost to the annals of time.

Straddling the worlds of Bombay and Calcutta through his writings, Nabenduda helps us relive that harsh yet touching past, with each story making us stop and ponder: what did the women feel when they had to sell their art, their hearts, and souls along with their bodies, within the short-lived span of their beauty and charm? He shows how they were exploited at every turn where they showed any sign of weakness. He evokes the pathos of lives that walked a tightrope until they could balance no more. And often that was how their saga faded, with no one turning to look back upon them.

As an artiste, I am particularly drawn to the story 'Song of a Sarangi'. The institution of courtesans always intrigued me as its study could address the cultural context of their arts. In times when society was culturally more evolved, the courtesan was the most alive source of enrichment. Beautiful and cerebral, Amiran of *Umrao Jaan* or Noor of *Jaanisaar* were always relevant in their times. They were a mirror of poetry and a muse for the poet. I would go so far as to say that a courtesan was the epitome of evolution and zenith of imagination. She was a true survivor in a man's world—a loser who never lost out, just went into oblivion with her fading glory. Today everything has gone to the lowest common denominator, hence the scope of an entertainer investing in poetry and the arts is no more viable. People who depict a courtesan too are contained by their own imagination and sense of culture, so they tend to drag it to the lowest common denominator.

Way before the moving image came into being, the courtesan was the muse for many a painter—from the folk-like depictions in Kalighat paintings to the fine miniatures of the durbars and the etchings of the colonial painters. And for photographers too. Daroga Abbas Ali and Mushkiruddowlah in their book, *Haseenan e Lakhnao*, glorified the courtesan beyond human imagination. The courtesan of Kashmir featured in Omar Khan's *Kabul to Kashmir* is equally evocative and alluring. That one little smile, that gentle stance captured by the play of light on her sensitive face made a courtesan immortal even as she faded into nothingness.

In *Jaanisaar*, set in 1875, I have introduced the advent

of photography through an English photographer who has accompanied our Indian protagonist from England to shoot the Delhi Durbar to show the might and majesty of Imperial India. Still, I feel that though recording and shooting had their relevance, they often inducted a mechanical ugliness and took the mystery away from the romance. It is the same with fabric: the romance and relevance of the handwoven, handspun went out of the window with the advent of machine-made yarn, and mass machine production has devoured tradition.

Ironically, though, it was the advent of technology—the development of sound recording and modes of reproduction—that made the song and the dance of courtesans, their music and poetry live on beyond their times. The gramophone record helped the passing on of traditional compositions that were hitherto handed down only from the heart to the heart, and saved it from being lost to the world.

The story of a woman living this predicament has varied through ages. Yet, no matter how the details diverged, it can be emphatically said that the lives of courtesans have been the mirror of a culture—'adab'. This 'adab' has been a central theme, the common thread running through the life that was a courtesan's way. Every other fact of her existence was secondary. However, underlying this was a strong current of insecurity. It varied in the different economic strata of society, but the traditional prototypes have been the same through the ages.

The wonderful part of this culture was its manifestation of a deeply spiritual and secular ethos, a true and organic blending of religions. Something the West would fail to fathom. Here, cultures were not just skin deep, they were a reflection of an ethos. Most tawaifs were devotees of Sufi saints. They observed forty days of muharram to commemorate the martyrdom of Imam Husain. Along with this, they celebrated the joyous union of Krishna and Radha as also the anguish of their separation. Muharram cleansed their souls and made their own sorrows seem minuscule before the tragedy of Karbala. It gave their voices a deep pain and their heart a wrenching poignancy. While Ali was the ascent of their spirituality, Govind was the epitome of their love and longing. The two coexisted seamlessly like nowhere else in the world.

It was this blending that gave thumri its soul ripping power which a courtesan blessed with sur could evoke. Thumri was the medium of poetry that the Sufi poets Hazrat Amir Khusrau, Hazrat Shah Niaz, Bedam Shah, Turaab Ali Shah, and the last king of Awadh, Wajid Ali Shah used to great effect. In Krishna, they found a commonly identifiable metaphor for their Pir. And the courtesan, with her intelligence and talent, became the fragrance of their art.

What is it in the institution of the courtesan that draws people into its fold? I have reflected upon this question and found only blurred answers. The answers come from these human lives where the highs are very high—as high as youth can ascend; and the lows are very low—as low as old age, disease and depravity can go.

The other reason that draws writers and film-makers to such lives is human helplessness. One is being born in it; another is being thrust into it. True, there are human failings and weaknesses in the realm of the courtesans too. For, it is a superstructure based on factors that become bigger by the day. And they change their face with the changing times. Yes, they swam in the river of flesh; but their world acquired a different dimension and they gained respectability because of their contribution to the arts. They became the muse, the emblem of the creative spirit.

In his stories, Nabenduda resurrects a persona, a time, and the characters around a protagonist who drive his/her life. And in doing so, he depicts a slice of reality around them. Each person is remembered by the beginning, middle and end that the writer has chosen for him or her. There is the relationship of Nemai Sen and Gauhar Jaan, from the time she gives her nath to him till he dies returning her nath back to her. Between these two moments they live a life of love that touches the deepest recesses of our heart. This love was beyond religion in every shade of its evolution. So too was the silent love of Uday Moinuddin and Hasina. Love was a zone of bliss beyond the manmade differences of the religious orthodoxy in which they breathed.

It was in this zone of purity that tawaifs and baijis expressed themselves, in words and melody. Their pain lived with them lifelong—only to become more and more beautiful with the growing pain. This pain, and the bliss of this pain, enriches every story in this collection.

MUZAFFAR ALI
New Delhi

Editor's Note

Tawaifs and Baijis, Wenches and Whores...

Chhaya. Tagar. Basana. Maanada-Panna-Radha. Hasina. Angelina. Gauhar Jaan... What do these ladies—all protagonists of this anthology—have in common? They are all engaged in sexual activity for money.

What are the sobriquets for them? Prostitute. Streetwalker. Wench. Call girl. Escort. Harlot. Hooker. Hustler. Vamp. Whore. Temptress. Tart. Puta. Fille de joie. Bawd. Moll. Courtesan. Lady of pleasure. Woman on the game. Lady of the night. Scarlet woman. Concubine. Paramour. Cocotte. Strumpet. Trollop. Wanton woman. Devadasi. Tawaif. Baiji. Ganika. Randi. Veshya...

This is less than half the seventy-five synonyms in the thesaurus for 'the woman of ill repute'. And this is without going into the term sex-worker, coined by Carol Leigh in the last century, which has seen people become 'porn star', 'sex educator', 'sexual trainer', and even 'actress turned prostitute'.

Where did the word prostitute come from? Is it from the Latin word 'prostitus', found since the 16th century? But the past participle of 'prostiture'—whether interpreted as 'to expose publicly' or read as 'thing that is standing'—does not have the abusive association the most ancient profession has. For that matter, the very phrase 'oldest profession'—a euphemism for prostitution when delicacy forbade the use of the word—is said to have acquired its opprobrious nuance only in the last lap of 19th century, after Rudyard Kipling used it in 'On the City Wall' (January 1889), a short story about an Indian prostitute. Kipling begins by citing a biblical reference:

> Lalun is a member of the most ancient profession in the world. Lilith was her very-great-grandmamma, and that was before the days of Eve as everyone knows. In the West, people say rude things about Lalun's profession, and write lectures about it, and distribute the lectures to young persons in order that Morality may be preserved. In the East where the profession is hereditary, descending from mother to daughter, nobody writes lectures or takes any notice; and that is a distinct proof of the inability of the East to manage its own affairs…

Several majors of world literature have gained from the narrative of such ladies: James Joyce of *Ulysses*, *Les Miserables* by Victor Hugo, Daniel Defoe's *Moll Flanders*, *Fanny Hill* by John Cleland, Shudraka's Sanskrit classic *Mricchakatika*, stories by Eugene O'Neil and Henri Maupassant, by Premendra Mitra or Bonophul in Bengali, and even Shakespeare's *Measure for Measure* come to mind immediately. And certain titles like *Threepenny Opera*, *Moulin Rouge*, *Belle de Jour*, *The World of Suzie Wong* are familiar because they lived on stage and screen.

So many more live with us through their forays on celluloid. Émile Zola's novel *Nana* was transcreated by Jean Renoir in 1926. George Cukor's *Camille* (1936) was born from Alexander Dumas's novel *La Dame aux Camélias* (1848). Federico Fellini's *Nights of*

Cabiria (1957); *Gigi* (1958) adapted from the 1944 novella of the same name by Collete; Billy Wilder's *Irma la Duce* (1963); Alan Pakula's *Klute* (1971); the Hong Kong movie *Intimate Confessions of a Chinese Courtesan* (1972); Martin Scorcese's *Taxi Driver* (1976); Louise Malle's *Pretty Baby* (1978); Rob Marshall's *Memoirs of a Geisha* (2005); Gary Marshall's super-duper hit *Pretty Woman* (1990).

Then there are the Indian classic movies on courtesans and nagar vadhus: K. Asif's *Mughal-e-Azam* (1960); Kidar Sharma's *Chitralekha* (1964); Lekh Tandon's *Amrapali* (1966); Kamal Amrohi's *Pakeezah* (1972); Girish Karnad's *Utsav* (1984); Muzaffar Ali's *Umrao Jaan*, made in 1981 and then remade in 2006 by J. P. Dutta; and again his recent *Jaanisaar* (2015). And our sluts? They too have an honourable existence in Bimal Roy's *Devdas* (1955), Asit Sen's *Mamta* (1966) as also *Sharafat* (1970); Chander Vohra's *Khilona* (1970); Shakti Samanta's *Amar Prem* (1972); Gulzar's *Mausam* (1975); Shyam Benegal's *Mandi* (1983); Sudhir Mishra and Anant Balani's *Chameli* (2003); Pradeep Sarkar's *Laaga Chunri Mein Daag* (2007); Srijit Mukherjee's *Rajkahini* (2015), remade in Hindi as *Begum Jaan* (2017). Before I exhaust this list, I must make a special mention of Buddhadev Dasgupta's *Mando Meyer Upakhyan* (2002). This movie was about a teenager whose mother, a brothel inmate, wants her to marry an old lech for money, but the rebel runs away to Calcutta, to find a new life in education.

Collectively, and continuously, these names underscore—whether fallen, shameful, sinful or not—the loves and lives of veshyas resounding through the heart of the world.

Here are some bare facts about the trade: if a person sells parts or organs of the body to mitigate hunger, we feel pity for them.

But if a woman sells her 'virtue'—another euphemism—we feel disgust. She is deplored, derided, disparaged. It is a grave sin to trade your virtue, even if it is to meet a societal need. So, for years the degraded woman could be booked under the law. In England of 1888, Jack the Ripper mutilated the sex organs only of women in prostitution. What is her crime, one may wonder? It is that men pay the 'shameful creature' for their sexual gratification.

Has any male ever hated the rag-picker or the jamadarni, the sweeper, who lives off the urban muck? Granted they are not accorded the front seat in social do's the way actresses are, but no one subjects them to visceral attack merely for being 'lowly' citizens.

Worldwide, whenever a 'fallen woman' is mentioned, people picture a siren who lures men into her den and then robs him of his wealth. Reality check: more often than not, she falls in love with a man who 'marries' her—sometimes he simply promises to—or impregnates her, takes her away from her home, and then dumps her; if not sells her to a brothel owner. True, some girls are in the profession by the fact of their birth: because her mother is a tawaif, or her father is a low-born natua. Is the 'husband' or the father ever made to pay for this form of economic exploitation? Not that I know of.

As a writer and a creative individual Nabendu Ghosh, to quote the iconic film-maker Mrinal Sen, 'never believed evil is man's natural state. Along with his characters he has confronted, fought and survived on hope.' This precisely is what we see in *Mistress of Melodies*. Be it Chhaya, the widow who is 'married' by Balram and deserted soon as she sells her jewellery to secure him a job; or Tagar, the virgin who is abandoned when she is with child; be it Basana, the orphan who wants to make a home, even if it is with a profiteer; be it Fatima, who takes money from Rustam and then attacks him with a scythe; or Hasina, the baiji who sells her adolescent daughter to the highest bidder and then finds out that he is the very man who sired the child: no matter how delicate or crude her status, this writer never looked down upon them. A Gulab Banu dances like a fairy; gramophone queen Gauhar Jaan sings like an angel; a dying Radha stands under the lamppost to earn the rent for her madam—not for a moment are they mere bodies bereft of soul.

Indeed, a part of their soul continues to pulsate even when they bare their bodies to loathsome, foul-smelling, fetid souls. That is why they have the icons of their gods in their dens. That is why Fatima cleans his wound when Rustam returns with a nasty cut. They offer money to the mate who is inhaling only to stop exhaling. They cook for their pimp.

Gauhar Jaan listens to the patriotic bard, Chaaran Kavi Mukunda Das, and stands up to the imperialists. This aspect, combined with the fact that she was the first Indian voice to take Hindustani ragas to the world stage, had fascinated the writer in Nabendu Ghosh. So he penned 'The Mistress of Melodies'—in English (the other stories are in translation)—as the first draft for a fuller screenplay. A major voice of 1940s in Bengali literature who moved to Bombay with Bimal Roy in 1951, this multifaceted author is more celebrated as the legend who scripted several classics of the Hindi screen through 1950s, 1960s, 1970s and 1980s.

As screenwriter too he trained the spotlight on the fact that a body can be stained, not the soul. '*Sharifon ka zamaane mein aji woh haal dekha ki, sharafat chhod di maine*' (When I saw the way the righteous conduct themselves in this world, I gave up righteousness) sang Hema Malini's character in *Sharafat* (1970). This blockbuster, wherein a feisty courtesan sets out in search of her father, was a satire on the hypocritical moral standards of the patriarchal society. Twenty years before this, Nabendu had written both the story and screenplay of *Baap Beti* wherein the little daughter of a 'dancer'—yes, one more euphemism—residing in a hostel sets out to find the 'father' she never had.

And talking of dancers, in *Chanda Aur Bijli*, adapted from *Oliver Twist*, she is a 'street singer'—a masked portrayal of a woman of easy virtue. Then, in the National Award-winning love lyric, *Teesri Kasam* (1966), dancer Hirabai falls in love with a naïve bullock-cart driver Hiraman who places her on the pedestal of a devi, and leaves the itinerant Nautanki company so as not to disillusion him. Who says that women visited every evening by hosts of men don't feel coy when they are taken for newly-wed brides! Certainly not Saadat Hasan Manto, the Urdu writer who was taken to court for writing about such ladies.

Nor did Sarat Chandra Chatterjee, the author of *Devdas* (1955). He created Chandramukhi, the beautiful and rich prostitute in Chitpore who 'disgusts' Devdas. The heartbroken protagonist, still pining for his childhood heartthrob Paro—who is married to an elderly zamindar—leaves the kotha but Chandramukhi does not forget his love for Paro nor does she undervalue it. On the contrary, she falls in love with Devdas, leaves her profession and devotes herself to him alone. Devdas is perhaps the first Indian film, then, in which a 'kothewali' is not hated but is an odd woman in love.

When I say, 'Chandramukhi leaves her profession,' I also ask myself: Is this really a 'profession'? When I hear the term 'sex-worker', I also want to know, 'Did this lady choose this as a career option? Did Chandramukhi apply for the job in a kotha? Do today's Radha-Maanada-Panna-Bunchi enjoy job security? Promotions? Retirement benefits? Was any one of the glamorous baijis counselled about the abuse inherent in the job? Does the housewife Chhaya, hurled into the job, have the option of quitting it? Can a Basana go for a career change?' Because the answer to all my questions are an emphatic no, I reject the 20th-century term that implies prostitution is innocuous, even wholesome work comparable to being a typist, or a dentist's secretary.

And long before I learnt to pose these questions, Nabendu Ghosh showed it is far from the truth. Yes, some—like Hasina—are born into the 'trade'. But most others are duped, cheated, sold, dumped to rot in the dungeons we know as brothels, with no escape in sight. Indeed, as 'Anchor' drives home with a shock, hunger is the devil that forces a simple housewife to sell her body to leches. Either she is feast for wild beasts or fodder for lusty animals. Fatima must let the moneylender claw her breasts; else, like Amina, jackals will tear out her flesh... The author, however, had a dream even for these ladies, and one night they muster courage to leave the darkness of the alley and walk towards a new sun. And one morning Rustam Ali, the sailor who only seeks flesh when his ship docks, finds the anchor of his life in a spunky woman.

Today—as perhaps always?—boys and transgenders too are prostituted. But women and girls still constitute the vast majority of those trafficked for sex. According to one estimate, in Europe alone 87 per cent of the humans in prostitution are women. Why? Perhaps because women are more vulnerable—physically, emotionally and most easily, economically.

However, even under these constraints, these ladies—tawaifs, baijis, nautankis, nautch girls—have been custodians and conveyors of India's classical arts. And that silver lining deserves to be saluted.

Ratnottama Sengupta
Kolkata

Mistress
of Melodies

Market Price

'O *Maa go*! What a scare you gave me!' Chhaya turned away her face, feigning anger.

'What's there to be scared of?' Balram smiled. 'I walked in to see you sitting quietly by the stove, lost in thought. All I did was ask, "What's bothering you?"—albeit in a false baritone. Is that all it takes to scare you? You jumped out of your skin, almost dropping the vessel on the stove. What a courageous woman I'm living with!'

'Okay, I'm a coward. Won't you get scared if, in an unknown city, you suddenly hear a strange voice speaking in your room?' Chhaya sat down next to the clay stove. This time she was truly put out.

The glow from the dying embers of the stove turned her face red. Beads of perspiration were clouding her forehead. They added to the allure Balram felt for her. He smiled as he bent forward to place before her the grocery he'd got from the market.

'All right, it's my fault. But don't look the other way, will you?' Balram pleaded. Chhaya didn't speak a word. 'Oh Chhayarani—'

Chhaya turned her face further away.

Balram moved closer to her and started reciting lines from a play:

> '*Why be petulant, darling? Why this pout?*
> *Why the film of tears in your eyes?*
> *Why this frozen eloquence?*
> *Why punish my small offence*
> *With rigid rejection?*'

Chhaya could no longer retain her stern composure—she dissolved into peals of laughter. 'Jatra again! Oh dear—'

'But you have to admit I have good taste. Here's the entire market at your feet: rohu, potatoes, tomatoes, cucumber, beans, chillies, lemon—'

'Enough! I can see for myself. You've ensured that you are made permanent in this role of bazaar sarkar, managing all household purchases.'

'Let me assure you, my lady, even if I lose this job I won't let go of such a pretty mistress!'

'My god! What a shameless bazaar sarkar I have on my staff,' Chhaya giggled.

'Honestly, my knuckles are aching from carrying your shopping bag,' Balram cribbed as he stretched out on the cot. 'Must have a cup of tea, Chhayarani!'

'Of course! I'll get it right away,' Chhaya smiled. 'But can we finish the accounts first?'

In a half-lying posture Balram lit a cigarette. 'Prices have gone up,' he said, letting out a mouthful of smoke. 'Potatoes—eight annas; six annas for the cauliflower, fish is Rs 3.50 a kilo, rice Rs 27 a quintal…'

'Oh god! Spiralling up with each passing day!'

'Sure they will. Aren't we a "developing" nation?'

'Developing nation? How?'

'Economics is just a notch above your head, pretty woman. Development means more money in people's pocket, and more money means higher prices—'

'Maybe,' Chhaya shrugged. 'But if prices go up at this rate, human life will become dirt cheap—'

'So what if it gets cheaper? Development is important. Therein lies the greatness of our nation—it doesn't lose sleep over the value of a few expendable men.'

'Get lost! Your words don't make any sense to me.'

'Why bother! There's enough time left for you to digest economics. For now, a fine cup of tea for me will suffice, beauty.'

Wearing an insincere frown Chhaya got busy with the kettle. Then she sorted out the veggies and washed the fish fillets. A child's cry wafted in from the next door. A Hindi film song was playing somewhere in the lane. A couple of sparrows had turned her windowsill into their playground.

'These fillets—how much are they, 250 grams?' Chhaya inquired.

Balram laughed aloud. 'That's what I told the fishmonger. "Be kind—instead of charging me for half a kilo tell me this is only 250 grams." But she just didn't agree—'

'Oh, so you've branded me a fishmonger!' Chhaya chuckled. Then turning serious, she said, 'But honestly, how will people survive? My mother used to say, after her marriage, when she first came to my father's village—you do remember, don't you? This was Gorajapur in Jessore district—a two-seer rohu would cost three or four annas. If it wasn't to your liking, just lower a net into the pond and haul a catch of three or four fish. Choose one and let the others go...'

Balram leaned on a pillow and fixed Chhaya with his gaze. She had already finished her bath. Her tresses, still wet, were tied in a loose knot at the end. A red line of alta was adding grace to her feet. Her longish, berry-shaped face wasn't exactly perfect. Nevertheless, it had something very appealing about it. Her well-formed body, too, was an intoxicant. Poor lady, Balram let out a deep sigh and focused on her words. This very Chhaya was initially so tongue-tied! And now, her happiness spilled over in words. Like one step leading on to another, one thought lead her on to another chain of thoughts, and then on to something else altogether.

'Did I tell you? This happened when the daughter of Bhattacharjee, the village priest, was to be married. He came and appealed to my grandpa and the old man fished out a maund of rohu from the pond and just gifted him that. Some days back I ran into a grandson of the same Bhattacharjee's daughter. He narrated the incident to me. In the course of our conversation he said—'

'Chhaya—'

'What?'

'The kettle's whistling away.'

'Oh god, yes!'

Chhaya hurried to pour the tea, handed the cup to Balram and went back to her cooking.

Balram cast a glance around the room. A single room with an adjoining verandah; even in this narrow lane of Kashi the rent was Rs 20 a month. Quite an ordinary room, but Chhaya's magic touch had transformed it into a tiny haven of peace. It had been about five months since they had set up this home, but already it held every household item one would need. A wooden charpoy, a cane chair, two mooras, mattress, pillows, mosquito net, cooking utensils, cups, saucers, glasses—nothing was lacking.

Balram's gaze returned to Chhaya. Again she was lost in her own thoughts. 'What are you thinking of, Chhayarani?'

A wan smile flitted over her face. 'Nothing…' she turned her face away from him.

'That's a lie. Thinking of home, are you?'

'No, no.'

'Come here.'

Chhaya smiled as she moved towards Balram.

'Tell me…'

Chhaya sat down next to him.

'Come closer.'

'No, I must return to my cooking.'

'Yes, I know that but tell me what's on your mind.'

'Nothing special, I was only thinking that all we need now is a job for you. We could then move elsewhere. This neighbourhood isn't very homely.'

'Why? Has anyone made any dirty remark?'

'No, why should they? But the other day that lady from No. 4 commented, "The two of you lovebirds make me green with envy."'

Balram smiled. 'What's bad about that?'

Chhaya pulled a face. 'It's so dark; you don't even get a glimpse of the sky.'

Poor soul, Balram thought to himself. The caged bird now wants to touch the sky once again.

'All right,' he spoke aloud, 'we'll move house.'

Chhaya suddenly placed her head on his chest and said, 'But when will you get to know about the job? It's been a week since…'

A cloud fell over Balram's face. He thought for a while before replying, 'We must wait for another fortnight. You don't land jobs overnight.'

'That's very true,' Chhaya immediately responded. 'Now we are provided for about a month, and still have a hundred and fifty rupees, right?'

Balram nodded his head.

'Oh god! That burning smell...' Chhaya jumped up and rushed towards the stove, grabbed the ladle and stirred the vegetables in the pan. 'You...make me forget everything...' she said as she kept stirring the vegetables. After a while she again looked towards Balram. He was quietly lying on the cot.

'Are you sleeping?'

'Na-ah,' Balram opened his eyes.

'Then? Lost in thought?' Chhaya walked up to the bed and sat near his feet.

'Again you've moved away from the stove? Want to serve cinders for lunch?'

'Oh dear, the gentleman is upset, I can see.' She tickled him under his feet. 'Please don't be in a rage, my lord!'

Balram didn't smile.

Chhaya frowned as she inched closer to him. 'Will you swear on me and tell me—'

'Tell you what?'

'What's bothering you?'

'Must you know everything?'

'Yes, I must.'

'No—'

'I must—or else...'

At this Balram turned to face Chhaya. 'It's this job I met those people about last week.'

'What about it?'

'They're demanding one thousand rupees for it. That's essentially to soften the head clerk. The job's not mine yet because I haven't come up with the money. Otherwise I would've got the job that very day.'

'One thousand rupees!' Chhaya's face lost all its colour. 'And if you can't pay?'

'No job then. It'll go to one of the others waiting with the money. I've sought a fortnight's time. Let me see what I can do.'

'Where will you arrange it from?'

'Don't know.' Balram sat up. 'Might have to steal or loot somebody.'

'Don't talk rubbish!' Chhaya raised her voice.

A hush fell upon the tiny room. Outside, a cow rushed down the gully. 'Run, run,' some coarse voices chased the cow. The sparrows perched on the window hadn't stopped chirping.

'Don't worry,' Chhaya consoled.

'What should I do then?' Balram's lips curved in a rueful smile.

'I still have my necklace, a pair of bangles, earrings and the wedding ring,' Chhaya spoke softly. 'Let's go and sell them.'

'What are you saying, Chhaya?'

'Precisely what I ought to. You get me a new set once you get the job. How can I be happy until I flaunt some jewellery gifted by you?'

'Just shut up! Don't ever speak such words, Chhaya. There's no question of selling your streedhan,' Balram looked away, putting an end to the conversation.

Chhaya had no more words to offer. She knew Balram better than to speak when he was upset. But why couldn't he understand? They simply couldn't carry on without a job. Chhaya burst into tears.

Her muffled cry drew Balram's attention. 'What's the matter?'

Chhaya looked away.

Balram moved up to her. 'Don't cry, Chhaya.'

'Don't speak to me!'

'Why don't you let me bear the burden of worry?'

'Is your problem different from mine? Have you thought about how to keep the kitchen fire going without a salary? Those pieces of gold won't fill my belly—' Chhaya succumbed to a fresh round of tears.

Arre…there she goes again. This time Balram started singing out his plea:

'Don't, dearest, don't
Shed any more tears—
They'll cause a flood
That might sink my heart…
Creation, even.
Your tears, dearest of mine,
Aren't raindrops
They're liquid fire…'

Chhaya smiled through her tears. Almost as if the sun had broken through the rain clouds.

'Get lost! Your theatrics only make me angry.'

'Why? Is it bad to be an actor?'

'You first answer me—'

'Answer what?'

'As if you don't know! I'm talking about the jewellery.'

'Look here Chhaya—'

'No, I'll start banging my head against the wall. This job is a must for us.'

'As you wish, then—' Balram again turned his face away.

At once Chhaya spread out her arms to fold Balram in an embrace. 'My precious!'

'But Chhaya,' Balram wiped the tears off her cheeks.

Unhesitatingly Chhaya shut him off with a kiss. 'No more ifs and buts,' she added busily. 'This very afternoon the two of us will go out. We'll sell off the jewellery so that you can confirm the job tomorrow itself. Is that clear?'

Chhaya didn't give Balram a chance to react. 'Not a word more,' she firmly said. 'After selling off the gold we will go on a tour of the town. Then we'll go for a movie. Tonight we'll dine out. I won't listen to any objection. We'll do as I tell you. Now hurry up and finish your bath…quick!'

Like an obedient child Balram stood up. He surrendered himself completely to Chhaya's whims. A strange game was signalled by the shut door in this sunless bylane of Kashi. The name of the game was love. When Balram came out of his bath, Chhaya took it upon herself to brush his hair. When they sat down to lunch, one fed the other. Instead of a siesta, Balram chose to entertain Chhaya with choicest dialogues from the jatras he'd watched or acted in, and she evinced her delight by repeatedly burying her face in his chest.

The housewife next door may've been listening in. She may've heard some of the lines but she surely couldn't witness this with her own eyes. The only voyeurs who could not be barred by the door or window were the sparrows—they kept up their chirpy commentary even as they got busy trying to build a love nest of their own in one corner of the air-vent high above the window.

As soon as the lazy afternoon rolled into evening, Chhaya commanded Balram to get dressed. She too dressed up for the outing. There was admiration for each other in their gaze. Chhaya sat on the floor to open her trunk and fished out her jewellery box. She placed it in a canvas bag and covered it with a scarf. She stepped out of their quarter, locked the door and strode up to keep pace with Balram.

'Why go around the market with so much gold?' Balram tried to protest.

'Shhh! Just walk with me in silence.'

'Okay, your wish…' Balram smiled.

When Chhaya was locking up her quarter, the sickly seven-year-old boy next door called out, 'Maa! Oh, mother!'

'What's it?' a rough voice floated out from inside.

'Come and take a look!'

'Quick!' Chhaya whispered. 'In no time she'll be at the door.' Before she could step into the lane the mother of five was at the door. In long strides Chhaya and Balram covered the distance up to the main road. 'Ooof,' Chhaya heaved a sigh of relief, 'there she was before one could say "presto". Are we some kind of museum piece?'

'Let them ogle—what's the harm?' Balram was willing to be charitable.

'Never!' Chhaya retorted. 'She's such a jealous woman—she can't bear to see me happy.'

They were on the main road now. The late-January sun was already setting on the horizon. They hailed a tonga and arrived at the market. A couple of hours later, with eleven hundred rupees in their pocket, they sat down on the wooden bench of a tea-stall and ordered a tea each.

'Don't grieve over the jewellery,' Chhaya tried to console Balram. 'We'll get new ones made.'

They finished their tea and made their way to a Hollywood

movie. They had dinner in a nice hotel. When they returned to their room, the clock struck ten.

The sound of the door opening automated the seven-year-old to whine: 'Maa, come sharp! They're back.'

'Quick!' Chhaya hurried Balram indoors. 'Hurry up.'

Before she could step inside, Lady Nextdoor was back at her watch. 'Witch!' Chhaya hissed, leaning against the wall.

'Chhee! Shame on you—' Balram didn't sound too pleased.

The minute he lit a matchstick to light the lamp, Chhaya blew it off. 'What's wrong with you?'

'Shhh! I want to say something to you.'

'Sure—but do we need the darkness for that?'

'Yes, I can't say what I want to tell you, except in the dark. Come closer. Where's your ear?' she groped in the dark.

Balram could feel her feverish breath as she whispered into his ears. Then she peacefully rested her head on his shoulder.

'Let go of me. I must light the lamp,' he wriggled.

'No. Why aren't you saying something?'

'I will. Let me first light the lamp, sweetie—'

As soon as Chhaya let go of him, Balram lit the lamp. Chhaya went and sat down on the bed. Balram walked up to her and held her in a fixed gaze. A smile kept playing on his lips.

'Don't—look—that way. I feel shy...embarrassed.'

'Chhayarani...'

'Yes?'

'You're the hue that colours spring,
The rainbow ribbon for the clouds
You put to shame the full moon
Oh lotus-bodied.
My heart quivers every time
My eyes stray to your face.'

'Ummm,' Chhaya gurgled.

'What's it?' Balram was puzzled.

'Acting like the hero of the film we saw today, aren't you?'

'Of course. I'll caress you all night.'

Chhaya moved a lock of hair from Balram's forehead. Peering into his eyes, she cooed—'I'm so happy today! Just wrap up the job, then we can move to another mohalla. But I'm warning you, it must have two bedrooms. You're looking at a salary of two hundred and fifty rupees a month. Surely we can afford thirty rupees for a two-room set up. Thirty for room rent, a hundred and fifty for household expenses, another ten to twenty rupees for the new member who'll join us... Even so, a saving of forty to fifty rupees shouldn't be difficult, right? What do you say, can't we?'

Balram nodded his assent. 'Yes, we can...rather, we'll have to. Shit!'

'What?'

'Must rush right away. I forgot to pick up cigarettes from the paan shop. I'll get it from the one at the end of this lane...' Balram opened the door and went out humming to himself.

Chhaya closed the door after him. On the verge of changing into her night clothes, she stopped before the mirror. No, she won't change: she'll spend this magical night in this cheerful Santipuri sari. Tonight is for celebrating. Ishh! She should have picked up some flowers. 'Forgetful, you!' she said to her reflection in the mirror. Never mind, she had a bottle of French perfume—she'll spray some of that on herself. Even better—she'll spray some on Balram too.

Chhaya succumbed to daydreaming as she lay waiting for Balram. Could she have imagined such happiness even a few months ago?

Chhaya had accompanied her mother when she had made her way to Calcutta after the Partition. She was married into a decently middle-class family. Her husband had a steady job in a factory nearby. But before she could notch up two years of married life, her husband died of smallpox. Her mother couldn't reconcile herself to Chhaya's widowhood: she too bought a ticket to heaven. With the little treasure trove left by her mother and her husband, and the uninhibited appeal of her uncontrollable youth, she was reduced to a slave in her brother-in-law's household. An aunt-in-law was her worst enemy. A couple of years later, her brother-in-law audaciously turned down every marriage proposal and started eyeing her greedily. Every time he spoke to her, his words were lined with double entendres. Initially Chhaya ignored his overtures. When she openly objected to his advances, her aunt-in-law uttered a single word: 'Slut!'

At this juncture a jatra group put up a performance in their para. *Kurukshetra*—the play was titled. Chhaya watched Balram play the role of Arjun. She was charmed. She was not oblivious to all that has been drilled into every Hindu widow down the centuries—but why had the words lost their edge? From the neighbourhood gossip Chhaya gleaned that Balram lived close by and, at that point of time, was unemployed.

One day she ran into him. Noting the deep curiosity in her eyes, Balram followed her to her doorstep. Then on, every single afternoon, when the aunt-in-law was enjoying her siesta and the brother-in-law was away at work, Chhaya would stand at her window—and find Balram keeping watch. At first she would shut the window. Later, she would leave it open.

One afternoon, from his post outside her window, Balram smiled at her. Another day Chhaya smiled back. Some days later, on the pretext of going to the Kalighat temple, Chhaya met him at Maidan. They spoke and spoke. After listening to her story, he proposed marriage. He urged her to elope with him. After a lot of conflict, and when she could no longer ward off her greedy brother-in-law's overtures, she resolved to join Balram. Yes, by now she too was feverishly anticipating the hour of their union. So one afternoon, when she stepped out, ostensibly to buy some household item, she took with her a bag containing some saris and her jewellery.

Once they arrived in Kashi, they spent a month in a hotel. Later they rented this place and moved in. They also quietly exchanged garlands in front of some gods. A local Brahmin Balram had arranged was the sole witness to this marriage.

Six months had passed since that day. Every effort to get a job—that had so far eluded them—would come to fruition now. 'Oh Lord Vishwanath of Kashi, please take mercy on us!' Since she met Balram, Chhaya had found a new meaning in life. Her Balram is Charm personified. But why was he taking so long to buy a cigarette? Must have struck up an adda with some stranger at the paan shop. Don't we know how he loves to chat with his friends!

Whose footsteps were those in the lane? Chhaya peeped out of the door. No, it wasn't him. Chhaya ruminated for a while, then put the latch on the door. Let him come back—she would teach him a lesson. She'll simply keep him waiting at the door. Balram will have to play out the appeasement sequence of 'Maan Bhanjan' in the Radha-Krishna jatra where He pleads guilty to Her and urges Her to relent and make love to Him.

Chhaya smiled to herself. She brought out the bottle of perfume from the chest. The tiny room was redolent with the heady scent that percolated into her consciousness and piqued her desire for his tight embrace. She sharpened the allure in her eyes with a fresh coat of kajal. Balram doesn't quite know the magnetic power of her sexuality…

At that very moment Balram was at the Kashi station. He bought a ticket to Kolkata, looked around to check if he recognized anyone, then lit a cigarette. Walking towards platform number 4 in order to board the last train to Mughalsarai, he kept planning his next move. Kolkata would be the best place to hide. It's easy to be anonymous amidst hundreds of thousands. He felt the inner pocket of his coat. Aah, the sweet sensation of currency notes! One thousand and one hundred rupees, almost. Enough to sustain him for the next few months. By then he would work out a new arrangement. Given the hard times they were going through, it was impossible to carry on an affair for longer than six months. The exchange of garlands? Huh! A mere ritual, a game of sorts, nothing more.

But Balram wasn't heartless. He'd left Chhaya with nearly a hundred and fifty rupees—and an enviable storehouse of sexuality. Surely her youth won't evaporate overnight, like camphor. Besides, he's leaving her in Kashi, the city of Lord Shiva. It's a holy city where thousands descend every single day for pilgrimage. The complex network of narrow dingy lanes…

Balram came to a halt on platform number 4. The signal was down, emitting a green light made hazy by the misty winter. Letting out a mouthful of smoke that lost its way in the darkness of the January night, Balram let out a deep sigh. Poor Chhaya! Such a sweet soul, she was. And so pretty. He was sorry to abandon the curious warmth of her firm, youthful body. His only consolation was that she'll stay on in his memories. The memories of intimate nights and playful days.

And Chhaya, too, won't easily forget him. The memory of Teenkari Das, aka Balram Chowdhury who charmed her as Arjun, will grow day by day inside her womb. It will continue to grow after it comes out of her womb. It will continue to grow and gnaw at her soul until her last breath. No, Chhaya will not forget Balram even if he forgets her.

Translated from the Bengali by Ratnottama Sengupta

Dregs

The rascal tried to hide.

The tram was crowded with office goers, but the kid could not evade my searching eyes. The tram company had suddenly become super vigilant, so the inspectors had no choice but to be strict. And the second-class compartment draws the worst of evaders, cheats, pranksters and con artists. Naturally I and my ilk, who are conductors in the second-class compartments, have to bear the brunt of the inspectors' snide remarks and caustic comments. Sometimes we put up a fight, a scuffle too now and then, I admit. How can I relax then? Or look the other way if I feel like it? The doctor has to heal himself first! Can I afford to lose a job in these trying times?

So I grabbed the kid by the scruff of his neck. 'What about a ticket, eh?'

The brat was not a bit scared. He simply grinned. Dark complexioned. Skinny. Five or six years old? A pair of black shorts, torn in patches; a shirt gone grey with grime; the skin hardened into hide with filth.

And a shiny pair of eyes, burning bright like a dog's. Wild, fearless. Why did this kid look so familiar?

'What are you grinning at? Where's your ticket?'

'Don't have one.'

'Why don't you have one?' My temper shot up. These rascals are a pain in the neck. Don't know where they're being imported from. Since the War ended, their numbers are multiplying by the day.

I relieved my anger by boxing his ears. 'Tell me why you don't have a ticket.'

Like a sudden bolt he hit me, and stared hard as he snapped back, 'Don't have any!'

'Why are you on this tramcar, then?'

'Will get off—'

'Will get off! Really? Before you do that I'll hand you over to the police…'

The passengers were enjoying this exchange. Some of them even spoke in my support. 'Yes,' one of them said, 'hand him over to the police. Or these dregs of society will grow up to pick our pockets, rob banks, mug us…'

'Chhora,' another passenger addressed the boy, 'don't you have any parents?'

The boy pulled a face as a glint of rage surfaced in his eyes. He didn't care to reply. But where had I seen this fellow?

'My, my! So much anger? Why don't you tell us, don't you have a father or a mother?'

'No!' He almost spat back. It was as if a cornered cub had bared its fangs.

The tram stopped at Jaggu Babu's market. I pushed him out of the car, 'Scoot!'

He got off, walked a few paces, then turned towards me and screamed, 'Shitpot!'

'Shut up!' I shouted at him.

The boy didn't budge. Instead, he screwed his eyes, bunched his fingers and punched the air with his fist as he retorted, 'I'll bust your skull, you rascal! I'll shit on your face—'

Livid, I tried to push my way through the passengers scrambling into the compartment. But the bell was sounded in the first-class compartment, and I was compelled to sound my bell too. The tram came alive on the track.

And as we surged ahead through all the noise and hullabaloo, the shrill voice of the six-year-old pierced my ears, 'Ay-ae you, bastard!'

He scampered alongside the tram to fling abuses at me. Finally he gave up. And that's when I could place him.

'See!' The passengers showered me with sympathy. 'See what a rascal the boy is!'

'Won't he be? Don't you see he doesn't know who his parents are...?'

Perhaps. But that kid had both, a father and a mother. I had seen them. At least, I knew his mother for months and years. Of course, I knew her merely by sight. As a tram conductor I used to see her board like any other passenger. When did she first board my tramcar...a few months after I joined this job?

The car crossed Elgin Road, then Theatre Road, and picked up speed. The wheels started a rap of their own. Keeping pace with the world around it, my tramcar started playing the drumbeats of a pakhawaj. And every now and then the cables overhead sparked thunder as if to mark a score. Swaying to and fro, winding my way through the passengers, sweating profusely in the sweltering heat, even as I handed tickets to the passengers,

I kept thinking of that kid's mother. I could recall every turn in the journey of her life…

I got this job right after I matriculated in 1942. I had scraped through the exams with great effort, after failing a couple of times. By this time our means were failing too. The faces of my brother and his wife would darken every time their eyes landed on me. So I gave up the idea of landing a secure white-collar job and climbed one rung down, socially.

Ironically that very year the clamour for freedom climbed a notch higher. As a tram conductor, I suffered the dual indignity of being a colonized citizen serving a company registered in London. At every step I feared the loss of the ruler's 'favour' too. Once in a while, the anger coursing through the country would lash out against the trams. It was during those rebellious days that I was initiated into the job. Then came 1943. The whole world was gripped by the madness of the World War II. The flames were dancing on our doorsteps. Death crossed over our threshold in the form of the Bengal Famine.

How many deaths did I witness? So many that I became indifferent. Every day, in the electric car, holding my own against heat and crowd, selling tickets even to evaders, I became a seasoned tram conductor. Still, a promotion eluded me. I continued seeing the world from a second-class compartment from morning to evening.

It was around that time. Was it July or August? The ceaseless downpour had led to water-logging on the streets by sundown. Due to the rains there were hardly any commuters that evening. So I gave my feet some rest and sat down to light up a bidi.

The tram stopped near Purna Cinema. A girl barely in her

teens stepped in, folded the umbrella that was shielding her from the downpour and sat in one corner.

The tram carried on its journey. The rain had veiled the landscape in a mist to further darken the grey evening. The glass shutters had been pulled down. So my eyes kept shifting from one passenger to another and came to rest on this girl. I felt like I had seen her somewhere. I focused my thoughts, and at once realized where.

These last few days this very girl had been riding the tram after sunset. She would alight at Esplanade. And return by the last tram late at night.

I looked squarely at her. Very young, but lacking the freshness that is natural in a teenager. Scrawny, bony, puny. An inexpensive but colourful sari was tightly draped around her yet-to-blossom figure. A string of beads hung around her neck, glass bangles tinkled on her wrist. A tightly wound bun on her nape indicated a wealth of cascading hair. A hint of talcum on her face and some ordinary fragrance sprinkled perhaps on her handkerchief… Nothing to merit a second look. But all in all, there was something grabbing my attention. It could have been her posture, the maturity on her face belying her green years, or an amazing luminosity in the dark of her eyes… I was, after all, a young man stepping into his twenty-second year, with unbridled manhood coursing through my veins. Lust was shadowing me at every footstep. But I had experienced the hardships of reality, and so I held it in a firm grip. Instead, I had developed an ability to understand the character of any individual simply by reading his or her face. This ability helped me decipher the story of this girl's waywardness.

Not Esplanade. But before that, just as the tram neared the

Indian Museum, the girl scanned to the right and left of the stop, opened her little umbrella and got off.

The elderly inspector Tarini Da was in my compartment. 'There goes one of them,' he observed as soon as she alighted.

'One of whom, Tarini Da?' I wanted to know.

'Pretending to be innocent, you slime!' Tarini Da got abusive. 'Haven't you seen these harlots?'

'Harlots? At this young age?' I feigned ignorance. One only stands to gain when Tarini Da is provoked.

'Young?' Tarini Da took pity on my gullibility. 'Everything is possible in Kalyug. And it's quite a norm in your country. Because your country has a king who does not govern. Because your country has people who are not really human. Besides, even selling their flesh does not prevent their dying on the pavement. In your country, even on a dark, rainy night these adolescents roam the streets in search of customers, and youths like you don't lose their sleep. You were not mothered by a woman, were you?'

'Certainly you were mothered by a woman, Tarini Da?' I could not help being sarcastic.

'Me?' Tarini Da shook his head. 'No. Besides, I am not a raging bull like you guys. Can't say I am a woman, either. I don't try to think of what I am... Day and night, day after day, I keep telling myself that I am nothing but an inspector in Calcutta Tramways Company.'

Esplanade. Without wasting a glance, Tarini Da strode off.

I sat brooding over what he had just spouted. The old man had roused such emotion with his words that, for quite a while, the clanging of the wheels on the iron tracks seemed to hammer in my head. I was ashamed of myself.

For the next few days I observed the girl. The same sort of

attire. She would board the tram at almost the same hour, at dusk; silently, with flagging steps. There was an air of melancholy about her. Dispiritedly she would stand or sit in one corner. Most of the time she would not even move, but every few minutes her unusually luminous eyes would scan the compartment from one end to the other. She, it seemed, was on the lookout for something, or someone. I would notice her searching eyes even as I issued tickets to sundry passengers. Those eyes did not spare even me, I felt them sizing up my body too.

A few days passed by.

That evening I was not on duty. So I went to visit my paternal aunt in Shyam Bazar. It was almost ten at night when I set out for home. I came down to Esplanade and was waiting for a tram to head up to Tollygunge. That is when my eyes fell on the girl. She was leaning against a pillar in the waiting room. I kept an eye on her, from a distance.

People were floating in, stopping by, chatting. A couple of men were pacing up and down nearby. Suddenly one of them, a middle-aged non-Bengali, noticed the girl, looked to his right and left, walked up to her, paused to fish out his packet of cigarettes and lit one up. He let out a ring of smoke, tilted his head towards the girl and said something. Slowly she turned towards him. The man spoke again. The girl turned her face away from him and headed straight for Curzon Park. The man stood there, dragging on his cigarette.

A tram for Ballygunge came up. A bunch of people rushed forward. The moment they had cleared out of my vision, I found that the man had disappeared.

Out of curiosity I walked towards Curzon Park. Quite right, I was! Even in the semi-darkness I could discern the outline of the girl. Walking alongside was the man. The two were proceeding towards the darkness of the solitary park.

I was reminded afresh of Tarini Da. His words were like a thorn in my skin. The bolt that charges our tramcars to slide along the iron track was once again coursing through my veins. I could sense a constant tingling in my fingertips. And yet, I could do nothing.

A week later. I was on evening duty. Again I spotted the girl. And at once I felt a surge of anger. Tarini Da was right: we are impotent. But the depths the country has reached cannot be set right overnight. Until then, shall we keep sliding down?

I looked disdainfully as I approached her with a ticket.

The girl glanced at me as she offered a two-anna coin and said, 'Esplanade.' Then at once, she looked away.

As I punched the ticket I asked her, 'What's your name? You look quite familiar...'

The girl looked back at me, the glint of a knife in her glance. But not a line on her face moved as she said, 'You don't know me.'

'Why don't you tell me your name?'

'No. You just hand me the ticket.'

'Every night you set out of your house—why?' I accosted her as I handed her the ticket.

'Why do you need to know that?' Sharply she raised her pitch.

'Don't you have any parent?'

'What does that have to do with you? Go sell tickets to the passengers—'

I was ready with an angry retort when a young man harshly cut in, 'Why are you interrogating her? Are you a policeman or an inspector?'

'Don't you see what she is?' I spat out in a stentorian voice.

'Do you hear that?' the girl hissed. 'Do you see how obnoxious he is?'

'Don't you dare!' The young passenger warned me. 'You'll be lynched if you speak like this to a respectable lady…'

A murmur of support filled the second-class compartment. I had to digest the insult.

The girl rose from her seat as we neared Jaggu Babu's market. She cast a momentary glance at the young man and got off.

Seconds later the young man followed her.

I could only grit my teeth.

Kalighat to Dalhousie. I saw the girl on my route on a number of journeys. The same expression: sad, silent, but with a calculated glance. I would turn away my face every time I spotted her. Disgusting!

One day, all of a sudden, I realized that the girl had not been taking this route. I heaved a sigh of relief. 'Good riddance!' I said to myself.

Then the calendar changed.

1944 dawned but the War continued to rage throughout the world. The horrendous famine had waned by this time. The lower rung of society, economically most deprived, had been wiped out. But hunger was now raiding the middle class. The quantity of rice on his plate had scaled down. The times, much like Duryodhan, were tugging at the attires of the women in these households that queued up in vain for rationed clothes. And they were all gearing up for a last-ditch battle for freedom from the imperialist rulers.

This determined assault had resonated in my ribcage too. I

felt stifled but could do nothing. My tramcar was running on its iron rails, spitting fire from its cables and singing its metallic song, shaking terra firma, keeping with the restless pace of the greats of the brand new world. And in its second class, I was peeling out tickets from a leather bag, punching them, handing them to passengers, counting every coin, sometimes after heated arguments, and forcing out ticketless travellers. In my attempt to cling on to the salary of fifty rupees a month, I had not had a chance to admire the Maidan in the twilight of spring, or on an autumn afternoon.

We had gone past autumn and were riding into winter. The northern wind was sending a chill down the spine. Even the woollen coat provided by the company failed to keep the chill out. The tram suddenly came to a noisy halt near Elgin Road. There had been an accident just ahead of us. Screams, shouts, cackle of voices. A full ten minutes later, the tram groaned back to life. That's when a young lady got into the tram.

As I walked up to her with the ticket, I was startled. Arre, it was that same girl! She had completely transformed. Her bony structure had filled out. She now had well rounded cheeks. And a light coat of lipstick added a veneer of glamour. She was tastefully dressed in a colourful handloom sari, her slippers were high-heeled, and her handbag was well matched.

'Ticket?'

'Five paise—' her voice too had turned mellifluous.

'Where to?'

She turned towards me. I realized that she had recognized me but she did not give that out. Looking the other way, she said, 'You just punch a ticket, why do you need to know so much?'

Suppressing my anger I handed it to her and moved away. She's prospering in her business! Clearly, she is a success in her sinful ways. Must say, she looks quite attractive now. Her lascivious lifestyle had lent an undefinable shine to the dark of her eyes. The curve of her lips, the slant of her neck, the sway of her hips were all sending out a 'come hither' message that no one would have any problem in decoding.

She got off at the very next stop. I stretched out my neck and saw her enter the first class. She is rising in life—so she is avoiding me. She won't go in second class anymore.

That day it didn't seem very glorious to be a second-class conductor.

Someone up there must have felt the pain inside me. Days later I was temporarily shifted to the first-class compartment on the Wellington–Gariahat route.

I started plying the new route with great enthusiasm.

Winter passed. New leaves sprouted to usher spring.

One day I saw her again. Not in the dark of night but in bright daylight. But why was she on this route? Was this also to eke out a living?

She had been rising steadily. Her affluence was showing in the crepe silk sari she was draped in. She looked fairer now, perhaps because of the make-up. And every piece of jewellery adorning her body was made of 22-carat gold.

She held her purse stylishly as she stepped into the compartment. Next to her was a healthy, dark-skinned man in his thirties. Rugged-looking, rough-tempered. Short cropped hair. Nattily attired in expensive clothes. Arrogant, unruly. You could see that he had made a killing in the black market.

'Ticket—' I went and stood near the girl.

'I'll pay,' the man said.

'No, I will,' the girl asserted.

The man laughed as he fished out a half-rupee coin from his pocket, tossed it in the air and asked the girl, 'Heads or tail?'

'Heads—' she chirped.

The man held out the coin in his palm and pretended defeat. 'Okay, you pay…' he said.

The girl giggled brazenly. She was oblivious of the tram packed with people. Laughing, she opened her bag, searched in a pile of notes, produced a tenner and turned towards me. She stopped laughing when she saw me. She had recognized me. I was witness to the first chapter of her life.

'Two, Chowringhee—' she said, turning serious.

I returned the ten-rupee note, 'No change.'

She pulled a wry face and arched her brows. 'Neither have I!'

All the bitterness I had stored up since that day when I was insulted because of this girl surfaced. 'What can I do? Why don't you carry change?'

I could see animosity in her eyes. She spat poison with her words, 'Why are you being repulsive?'

I lost my calm at this affront. 'Beware of what you say! I know you—'

Within a second the dark-skinned man jumped at me, 'Shut up, you bloody swine!'

Without any warning a blow landed on my cheek. I lunged forward. The passengers cried out in unison. Inspector Idris Mian intervened. Everyone held me responsible. In order to save my job I had to apologize to the girl and the man. Still I could not reveal her reality. And even if I had, who would have believed me? Wealth buys you respect everywhere in the world. If you are rich, if you have money, even thieves are venerated and lechers canonized. Who will pay any heed to what is said by a man whose life breath depends on a 60-rupees-per-month job?

The incident did not drag on. Idris Mian had to file a report although he tried to mitigate my culpability. I continued in the first class but it became clear that I would have to return to the second class at no notice.

I stored up some more gripe in my heart. The desire to avenge this insult kept growing within me. Surely I would get a chance to get even. Once more, I mulled over Tarini Da's words. No, there is no point in feeling sorry for these sluts.

Spring had dissolved into summer when I saw her again. Saw them—together.

What's this? The girl had sindoor in the parting of her hair? No, I was wrong. She was wearing a vermillion bindi only on her forehead but not in her parting. Cultivating the looks of a housewife!

Certainly they recognized me. But today there was no friction.

I had this urge to eavesdrop on their conversation. I tried, too. Ordinary, mundane exchanges. Saris. Movies. Servants and helps. And the new contracts the guy had been promised.

I was quite taken aback. The girl was speaking ceaselessly.

When they got off the tram, I noticed that the girl was pregnant. Surprise! What more will come to be!

And then again I did not see them for days, weeks. By the time I saw them next, it was 1945. The New Year was still new. I was plying the Tollygunge–Dalhousie route—back to the second class! This time, the girl had a baby in her arms. A boy. The man was next to her but she looked rather spent. Tired. Her health had dwindled. The man was also not in a chatty mood—he kept largely to himself, sombre, sullen. I could not make out much more from my post.

Sigh. Regret. I was back here in the second class but before I could settle my score with the girl. I felt small. Impotent. Life had not given me the satisfaction of putting her in her place…

The War ended. The market turned damp for contractors. The tribe of unemployed was expanding in so many different fields. Agitation. Action. The waves of unrest were often directed towards the trams. Before long, another New Year was upon us.

Somewhere in the midst of all that turmoil I spotted the girl. In broad daylight. In Tollygunge. She was standing at one of the stops, holding a one-year-old child in the crook of her hip. She moved towards the first class, then retraced her steps and got into the second class. Today she was not accompanied by the man.

'Ticket—'

The girl looked at me. There was no fire in her eyes! Instead, there was a hint of sadness in her movement as she lowered her face, opened her purse and took out the coins. 'Bhowanipore, one—'

'Why not Chowringhee?' Poison spilled out as I could not curb the temptation to strike at her.

'No—' she did not lift her face.

'Where's the bloke?'

'Who are you talking about?'

'Who was with you the other day?'

'My husband—' she lifted a weary set of eyes towards me.

What's wrong? Why was I missing that fire in her gaze? And why had she withered thus? Fewer pieces of gold on her, yes. And the cotton handloom did not show her off the way her crepe silk did. So what's cooking?

'Husband?' I poured levity in my voice. 'Oh yes! So then, where is the gentleman?'

'At work.'

'At work?' I mimicked her. 'Or taken to his heels?'

Clearly this touched a raw nerve. There was acid in the air as she spat out the words, 'Do you really want me to scream?'

A wildness flickered in the dark of her eyes. I was stumped, but I pretended to care two hoots and moved away in the opposite direction. No point in provoking her further. But I was certain I would soon have the opportunity to even out the insult.

She had risen, step by step, in her business. Now she had started descending, step by step, in life. Once again she had that doleful air about her.

The riots started in a matter of days. Satan had unleashed a whirlwind of fury and hatred. On the streets of Calcutta, Hindus and Muslims played Holi with each other's blood. Bullets. Acid. Bombs. And the city was trembling in the throes of fear. Day and night. Amid all this came the Tram Strike. Through all this, 1946 melted into 1947—and the nation geared up for the Partition. And, with that, more frustration came to layer the palpitations and heartburn.

I had been working for five years. I was nearing twenty-seven but was far from the thoughts of marriage and family. Why, I did not even garner the confidence to nurse a love in my life! Why would I? It would only add to my stress and agony, not ecstasy. It was perhaps better to turn a blind eye to the fact that every man needs a woman to liven up his existence on this planet. Better for the poor of this world to follow the ideal of sacrifice, and celibacy, and leave the charms of feminine company to the moneyed lot. They will make the most of it, and then some more.

One evening when I was revelling in such bitterness, I saw her again.

'Ticket?'

'Six paise—Esplanade.'

I looked at her. 'Esplanade!'

She nodded and gave a wan smile.

I gritted my teeth. Just you wait, you wench, I will soon get to settle that old score with you.

But how ungainly she had turned! And all the gold was gone from her body, save those rings clinging to her earlobes. The glass bangles were back on her wrist, beads around her neck...

She got down at Esplanade. And then again I did not see her for countless days.

Sprinkling splinters of fire and creating waves of sound on the iron tracks, when my tramcar would race past the Maidan, thoughts of the girl would suddenly flicker in my mind. Perhaps the Maidan caused the association. The velvety stretch of green, basking in the warmth of the soft winter sunlight, would trigger thoughts of what goes on when darkness falls. Perhaps the girl still walks in there to seek the veil of facelessness. Perhaps she courts a coolie standing at the corner of Chowringhee, or the company of some driver, and takes them to a nook in some corner of the wide green stretch, then gets overly friendly with them, and...

'Ticket? Have you got one? And yours sir?'

Tring tring...

My tram races ahead.

Days, nights. Nights, days.

The tram races on. I listen to its duet with iron rails and electric cables and feel empowered. This new-age chariot asserts every passing day that, unless you are hard like iron, and as determined, as electric-willed, you will not get anywhere in life.

Days have gone by, unnoticed, altering me bit by bit.

Days have gone by, without catching the sight of her. I got the feeling that she had been avoiding my travel time and taking other trams for her nocturnal adventures. I had, after all, partially witnessed the tragic story of her rise and fall. It would be natural for her to not reveal herself before me.

But we met again. In 1949. Midsummer. Late at night. I was homeward bound, for Ballygunge. As soon as the tram set out from Esplanade a wild dusty storm raged in. My tram was not to be outdone, though. Perhaps the storm had set off one in the heart of the driver Ram Birij. But as it reached the Indian Museum, someone raised a hand to request a stop. The tram stopped. A woman stepped in, and the coach was back in motion.

'Ticket—'

She shook her head, 'No money—'

'No money? Then why did you board?' I snapped in reply.

The woman turned towards me.

Perhaps because of the storm my tram was spitting more splinters of fire than usual. I had dust in my eyes. Still, I made no mistake. It was her.

'You!'

'I'm very late today, but I must get home—'

I had stored up layers of insult deep within. It spilled out now. 'Your paramour of two days had slapped me, you may have forgotten that—'

'Forgive me, Dada!'

Dada! Did someone hit me with a hammer?

'Haven't earned a paisa today,' she spoke on. 'And the kid is down with fever, I must…'

She started to cough. I looked at her. Not only had she turned scrawny, she had suddenly aged too. She was back to the angular body of six years ago, but, back then, she had age on her side.

Today she had little to commend her. She was draped in a coarse piece of cloth, and with no piece of adornment whatsoever on her.

'Dada…?'

'Sit,' I gave her my assurance. And with that the storm seemed to miraculously cease within me. The clanging of the wheels against the iron tracks seemed to alter its harsh intonation.

The girl sat down in that old familiar posture of melancholy and pain. Passengers boarded the tram, they purchased tickets from me, I counted the coins and handed back the change, they got off. And through all this, in bits and pieces, I gathered the story of her life. For seven years I had been confronting her, but how little I knew about her!

Her name was Basana. Her mother had passed away a long time ago. Her father, who worked in a carpenter's shop, had died of typhoid. She moved in with her sister at Bhowanipore. The brother-in-law was engaged in a motor-manufacturing company. As luck would have it, he too fell to cholera. Darkness engulfed the world of the two sisters. Her didi had already mothered three kids. How to feed them? Both the sisters had to come down to walking the streets. The two would go in two opposite directions. Such goings-on in the neighbourhood would have driven them out of their society!

It had continued thus for a while when the tide turned. All of a sudden Basana could entrap Prince Black Marketeer. A concocted tale led him to believe that she was a virgin in the field. He put her up in a separate flat. But the trader was keen only to have a good time. As soon as the kid came along he lost interest in her. And then one fine day he disappeared. Again she was on the streets.

Ill-fated Basana had sincerely wanted to set up a home and raise a family with the man. So his disappearance left a deep scar on her. One by one she sold off all her jewellery and before long all her money was gone. And she lost her health. Following a massive fight with her sister, she started to live separately. But by now she had contracted an incurable disease. In spite of it she would go out every night. Somehow things did not work out. Maybe because she was ailing.

She started coughing a dry cough. Tears were streaming down her cheeks. Kalighat.

'See you, Dada—' she got off.

Leaving her behind in a whirlwind of dust we charged ahead, spilling fire on iron rails. Suddenly it seemed to me that its Clang-Clang-Clang had changed into Dada-Dada-Dada.

I saw her two more times.

The first was in broad daylight. Near Chittaranjan Seva Sadan, with her son. That was a long time ago. The boy must have been five. Bony, tearful.

'May I board, Dada? I am running a temperature, can't walk anymore…'

'Get in.'

She climbed in and kept standing in one corner, hesitant to occupy a seat.

'Take a seat,' I told her.

She sat down, in that dour posture of resignation and sorrow. The eyes had lost their sharpness. They were dead, dull eyes. She kept coughing intermittently, her gaze fixed out of the window.

The boy kept whinging all the way down, 'When will you give me food? I'm hungry! Tell me, when? You witch—'

The girl did not protest, she simply stared on. No word. No movement.

The last time was near Purna Cinema. She was squatting on the pavement with her son. The kid was begging. 'O babu—dying of hunger. I am! Babu, O babu—'

A few seconds. Then the tram took off. I did not look back. I'd recall the word 'Dada'! Better not to…

I did not see her ever again. But I did see the boy some six months later. In 1950. A constable boarded our tram at the corner of Kalighat, holding the boy by his hand.

'What is the matter, sir?' The passengers were curious. 'Has he picked someone's pocket? Or stolen something?'

'No, no. His mother was lying dead.'

'How?'

'Illness. She was lying dead in the shanty, and the kid was crying away copiously. I am taking him to the thana to file a report.'

'So what happens to the kid now?'

'He has an aunt, it seems. I will take him there. Surely the government cannot be responsible for all the orphans in the nation!'

'Of course not, sepoy sir! How can it?'

Six months ago, the boy was shedding tears. Today, he was dry-eyed.

Strange. The girl was dead! I had been seeing her for almost a decade. It was as if I had known her all her life.

Dada! Dada! Dada! I could hear her voice in the sound of the tramcar. But I could do nothing. I simply turned my face away from the boy.

That very boy. He showered a vocabulary of abuses on me as he got off the tram. But where does he live? With his aunt? Certainly not. He lives on the streets, pavements, the veranda of someone's house, courtyard of another's… Like a pariah dog. Or a sewer rat.

The tram stopped. I am on my return journey from Dalhousie to Ballygunge.

'Ticket—'

A girl turned towards me. 'Kalighat,' she answered. I recognized her as I handed her the ticket. The same look of sadness deep within her eyes. Another girl like Basana. Basana is dead but her tribe is growing by the day.

I turned away, and gritted my teeth as I listened to the soulless song of the iron rails. Fire wanted to splinter out of my fingertips. But all I could do was absolutely nothing.

Only, I went near a passenger and unduly screamed, 'Ticket? Where's your ticket?'

Translated from the Bengali by Ratnottama Sengupta

Song of a Sarangi

I

Nineteenth-century Calcutta. Some time after the Sepoy Mutiny. The rule of the British law had been well established. 'Babudom' had become well entrenched. By this time certain neighbourhoods of Calcutta such as Chitpore and Bowbazar had become home to a group of professional singers and dancers called 'baiji'. These girls came from north India and almost all of them were Muslims.

Soon after sundown, the rich and wealthy seths and babus of the city would come in their carriages and step into the kothas of these baijis. In a large hall, tastefully appointed with erotic images of nude and semi-nude women, they would recline on the soft mattresses spread out on the floor. And leaning on colourful velvety bolsters, under the dazzling light of multi-tiered chandeliers, they would sip whisky from crystal glasses as they delighted in the performances of these nautch girls.

One tawaif might sing, '*Baagon mein phool khile, Hum tumko na bhuley* (Every flower that blooms reminds me of you...)'

Another would sing a Kafi thumri, '*Shyam ki muraliya sakhi,*

Baj rahi ban mein (Listen to that magic flute! Krishna is playing in the forest.)'

Yet another baiji would sing, '*Piya mor pardes*'—

'My beloved is away.
The days are unending, the nights bottomless.
In my lonely bed I toss and turn,
Sleepless and lonesome…
Oh merciless beloved!
You are away in a strange land.'

The baijis would sing and dance to the newly invented harmonium—a cross between an organ and a reed—which had become immensely popular as it would enhance the appeal of the performance. The rhythmic beat of the tabla would send them into a trance and they would whirl with abandon.

The beauty, the erotic expressions and gestures, perhaps also the coquettish airs of these nautch girls, mesmerized these tycoons. As their alcohol-tinted eyes devoured the defiant bosoms and slim midriffs, the playful looks of the kohl-lined eyes, and the sudden thrust of those hips, they would get aroused with lust. The moment the dancers arrived at the pause of sam—the first beat in a taal—they would break into the chorus of 'Wah! Wah! Well done, Bai! Bravo…' And with this, they would put their hands into their pockets to shower the dancers with money, which the ladies would carefully pick up, bow low, and thank the men saying, 'Tasleem!'

The mujra would come to an end after midnight. The barons, the zamindars, the babus, the seths and their hangers-on would then trundle home. On occasion, as per an arrangement with the madam, a babu would stay back. Then the chandelier would lose its brilliance, and its place would be taken by the dim light of a lamp. Losing himself in its light, a sarangi player sitting outside the baiji's bedroom would strike the romantic notes of the night-time raga, Khamaj, to match the mood of the couple united inside in a lusty embrace. Were words to be added to the melody of the strings, they would say, '*Shyam, mori maano batiya, Aaj ki raat mat jaao* (Pay heed to my pleas, O Krishna! Don't go home tonight…)'

The house of Hasina Baiji of Chitpore is buzzing with activity today. The mujra hall is already studded with six babus and seths. Looking after them and serving their needs are Hasina's friends: Gulshan Baiji and Roshan Baiji. Hasina's handmaiden Rabiya is assisting them. Sitting at the far end of the room, man-servants Banda Hanif and Ismail are swaying two giant palm-leaf fans with ornate borders, providing relief from the sultry heat. At the other end are the musicians: fifty-year-old tabla player Naseer Khan; forty-five-year-old Jhaanu Mullick, an expert harmonium player; and the forty-year-old sarangi player Uday Moinuddin.

What have they assembled for? What is the buzz about? It is for the nath-utarna ceremony. Today Hasina's daughter, the fifteen-year-old beauty Gulab Banu, will be auctioned off. It is a 'wedding ceremony' for the daughters of the baijis, distinct with its own set of rites and rituals. A nath—nose ring—is fastened on every girl who attains puberty. This nose ring is taken off only by the man who acquires the right to 'marry' her, and on the first night of 'marriage' deflowers her. Only then does she gain acceptance as a baiji and can enter the profession and make a living off her singing and dancing. This 'husband' who removes her nath may visit her for a few days or weeks but cannot claim her forever.

The good fortune of deflowering a virgin can be an expensive proposition. But many a loaded seth, wealthy businessman, and moneyed babu drool at the prospect. So there is stiff competition. Today they will compete to determine who is fortunate enough to ravish Gulab Banu. In other words, there will be an auction that will show how far one is willing to go for this 'good fortune'. The one who bids highest will be the first honeybee to suck the innocence out of Gulab.

The ones sipping sherbets as they wait to bid at the auction are the eminent decadents of the city. The first one is Bishu Seth, an obese iron merchant, around forty-five years old, with an obscene paunch and the sly look of a jackal in his eyes. He lost two wives, one after the other, and now lives a widower's existence.

Second in line is Keramatullah Khan, not less than fifty-five years old, of medium build, chubby looks, ordinary appearance but well turned out. This silk trader has two wives living under the same roof.

Vindhyeswari Prasad, the third, is a dandy with three gem-studded rings on his fingers and the look of a contented, healthy and happy man.

Janakinath Basu, the fourth, is a rice merchant nearing fifty years of age. Tall, lanky, his eyes spinning this way and that, he cohabits with his sister-in-law ever since his wife passed away.

Ramram Dutta, the fifth, has the typical look of a babu. At fifty-two, he wears long hair, dons a pleated dhoti and a kurta of superfine cotton. A giant red ruby shines on the index finger of his right hand. He is a zamindar of vintage ancestry, but with a wife who is forever ailing.

Qasem Khan, the sixth, is a recent import into Calcutta.

Yet, reports of his wealth have already made inroads into the Bengali society and the ranks of baijis. He made his fortunes in the Punjab, they say. Now he is here to trade in diamonds and gems. Almost fifty years old, he has a charming appearance: thick brows, a well-maintained beard and moustache, a few pockmarks distinguishing his forehead and aquiline nose. Well-fed, standing tall on his feet, dressed in a Pathan-style pyjama suit, the diamond and pearl on his right hand indicate the dominant positions of the Venus and Moon in his birth chart. But about his family, few know anything for sure. They only know that this gentleman loves to see his friends drink till they are sozzled.

This evening's auction will be conducted by another baiji: forty-five-year-old Kulsum Bai. Hasina treats her like an elder sister born of the same mother. She has the personality as well as the power to be a leader. This Kulsum Bai now enters the hall, bows to the assembly of wealthy men and says, 'Your lordships! Allow us to start the proceedings. We will begin with a thumri by Hasina Bai and as she sings her daughter, Gulab Banu—today's star—will appear briefly and salute you all. Once Hasina concludes her performance, we will begin the auction. Do we have your permission?'

The assembled deep pockets spoke in almost a chorus: 'Sure, sure…'

'Most certainly.'

'Let us get started.'

'Accepted.'

'Without a doubt!'

Kulsum Bai bows once more, then looks towards the musicians and smiles sweetly. 'Let's begin, ustads.'

Promptly Jhanu Mullick presses the reeds of the harmonium

and creates the sound of a jaltarang. The tanpura resonates at the fingers of the aged Sagiruddin. The sarangi resounds at Moinuddin's touch. The quiet, charming man has dreamy eyes. And from his sarangi come the sublime melodies.

Now Naseer Khan hits the tabla to play a rela that makes all the deep pockets sway to the beat.

'Wah wah! Bravo—'

'Well done!'

'Subhanallah!'

The minute the fast-paced tabla solo ends, the jingle of ghungroos announces the arrival of Hasina Bai. She circles her way into the room, comes to a halt in the hall and bows to the gathering: 'Tasleem!'

The deep pockets raise their hands to acknowledge her obeisance.

Now Kulsum Bai speaks. 'This is a significant day in Hasina's life. Today her only child, her dear daughter, the light of her eyes will be auctioned!'

'Congratulations, Hasina Bai! Well done—'

'May her heart's desire be fulfilled—'

The musicians play on and Hasina dances on. The looks she is casting—mesmerizing! Her smile, the captivating rhythm of her undulating body, every moment they assert that she is 'The Best' in the market.

All of a sudden another set of ghungroos announces itself. Riding on its sound, a lithe fifteen-year-old lifts the curtain and enters the floor, dancing and smiling a coy smile. One by one she looks into the eyes of the gentlemen, and her rousing smile sends the blood racing in their veins.

Kulsum Bai announces in a singsong tone, almost in sync

with the beats of the tabla, 'Gracious presence! This is the light of Hasina Bai's eyes, her dearest darling, her pride—Gulab Banu! It is in her honour, to announce her coming of age that you have all gathered today.'

Gulab twirls to the music and at every pause in the beat she salaams each of the six men, her mother, and the four musicians. Then she completes a pirouette and bursts into a song. At once Uday Moinuddin's sarangi too starts singing. Shyly Gulab emotes the nakhra, the coquetry of the song, '*Abhi umar mor bari* (I am of an innocent age…)'

Moinuddin's sarangi too resonates the naughty plea of the innocent virgin. *Umar mor bari…na chhedo mohe kasam tumhari.* There is enchantment in their voices when the listeners praise the opening lines of the song: Do not—pray, tease me not with your tight embrace… Tender is my body, you will crush every bit of me. Adolescence has yet to endow me with robust youth. I am still new and uninitiated in the ways of love… O skilled lover, I am not yet aware of the rules of the game you long to play with me—*Abhi umar mor bari…*

The applause gets more and more rapturous.

'Devastating!'

'God's perfection.'

'Glory to Him for this spark of fire.'

'May you live long, darling…'

Hasina now recedes to the background and stands watching alongside Kulsum Bai, while Gulab holds the floor, singing and dancing all by herself. The deep pockets watch wide-eyed, getting increasingly mesmerized by her honeyed voice and her darting glances. Intoxication is getting the better of them every time her luscious lips break into a smile; with every twist of her slim waist, every thump of her buoyant breast. Their style varies as per their backgrounds, their tastes and upbringing, but every one of them is already undressing her in their minds. Gulab Banu keeps singing as she dances on—*Abhi umar mor bari*—I'm scared, my heart quivers, my body quakes... Do not, O do not touch me, fold me not in a tight embrace... You be the protector of my modesty, I am still innocent...

'Wow! How delicate!'

'Delectable! Angel from Heaven.'

'Sublime—this dance.'

'Music of paradise... Divine!'

The tabla breaks into a rela. Gulab recreates the rela with her single ankle bell. The rela completed, Gulab comes to a halt but Uday Moinuddin's sarangi does not stop. In tune with it Gulab circles the hall, courteously salaaming everyone individually. 'Aadab!' Then, with a burst of laughter she parts the curtains and disappears behind them.

'Damn! The bird has flown away,' Bishu Seth regrets. The other men laugh in agreement and variously respond: 'What delicacy!'

'Delightful elegance.'

'Allure personified.'

'Worthy daughter of Hasina Bai—'

Kulsum Bai steps forward. 'So gentlemen, do we have your permission to start the auction now?'

'Yes, yes, sure—'

'Let's get going.'

'Action!'

Kulsum Bai sits down to face the gathering with Hasina right behind her. The musicians depart from the room respectfully. When Uday Moinuddin is about to step out, Hasina's handmaiden Rabiya thirstily looks at him. The servant Hanif also leaves as he is gestured to, by Hasina.

Kulsum Bai looks at Bishu Seth, 'Why don't you start the bids, sethji?'

Bishu Seth smiles. The sly fox inside the dark of his eyes may have whispered something to him; he says, 'Well, then, here's my bid: five thousand rupees.'

Kulsum scans all the faces, then says, 'You've just seen Gulab. She is allure personified. Whether in dance or in music, she has done her teachers proud. Above all is her beauty. It justifies her name. And she is no ordinary rose. She is a Basra Gulab. You have pegged this priceless rose at a mere five thousand rupees? I'm saddened to hear this. Who will relieve me of my sorrow?'

Ramram Dutta raises his hand to offer, 'Ten thousand rupees.'

Kulsum shakes her head, 'No, no, sirs! This is not honouring Gulab.'

Now the short-statured Vindhyeswari Prasad lifts his hand adorned with three gem-studded rings and speaks aloud, 'Twelve thousand Kulsum Bai—'

'In the bazaar of beauty, you should not utter such measly figures!' Kulsum Bai smirks. Immediately the fox jumps out of Bishu Seth's eyes. 'Thirteen!' he raises his voice.

But before he can finish, silk-trader Keramatullah Khan raises his pitch to a higher octave to beat Bishu Seth, 'Fifteen thousand rupees, baiji!'

The lanky Janakinath Basu is not to be left behind. He sits upright and says, 'Sixteen thousand—'

Keramatullah tenders, 'Seventeen thousand rupees!' Janaki shouts, 'Eighteen th-ou-sa-nd!' Vindhyeswari Prasad folds his palm into a punch and screams, 'Nineteeeeen…'

Babu Ramram Dutta's ruby ring flashes in angry brilliance. So far he has been reclining on a velvet bolster. Now he bolts upright, smiles and softly intones, 'I will close at twenty.'

Silence descends in the hall. The Bengali Babu surveys the room, a smug smile in place.

Kulsum says, 'Graciousness, Gulbanu is a rosebud of such beauty that she's peerless even now. Imagine how much more intoxicating her fragrance will be when she matures! For such a refreshing young girl, even twenty thousand is too little. Won't one of you be gracious enough to bid higher?'

Silence. No one ruptures it. The smile on Ramram Dutta's face, too, is not fractured. Kulsum pans her gaze from one end of the room to the other, to focus by turn on the six. Everyone seems to have opted out of the race. Save Kulsum. Rice, then, cost four rupees a ser. Clearly twenty thousand is a lot of money. Still, what's wrong with trying to earn a bit more?

Kulsum looks around. Qasem Khan, the crorepati who has made his fortune selling diamonds, has not spoken even once. Why hasn't he made a single bid? Does he not like Gulbanu even a little? Strange. There is no trace of emotion on his sphinx-like face.

Ramram Dutta gets impatient. 'What's on, Kulsum Bai? Why waste time when no one is inclined to bid any higher? Speak your mind.'

This forces Kulsum Bai to close the proceedings. 'Twenty thousand one—'

She pauses to glance around once more. 'Twenty thousand two—'

Now Qasem Khan spreads the glitter of his diamonds. His baritone voice musically rings out, 'Thirty thousand rupees, Kulsum baiji.'

'J-j-i?' Kulsum stutters.

'Thirty thousand rupees,' Qasem Khan repeats.

Now Kulsum beams. And Hasina Bai breathes easy.

'Thirty thousand one—'

No one utters a word.

Kulsum raises her pitch, 'Thirty thousand two—'

The five deep pockets grit their teeth and hold back their words. Kulsum Bai is almost screaming now. 'There's still scope to raise the bar. I will only be happy to count all over again. Go on! Speak now, if you want to, before I say thirty thousand... thirty...thou-sand...' Kulsum pauses but no one interrupts the count. Kulsum has to conclude, 'Thirty thousand—three! End of auction.'

She looks around the room. 'Shukriya meherbaan! This precious moment has made it clear that the newcomer in Calcutta's culturedom, diamond merchant Qasem Khan Saheb will be the one to deflower Gulab Banu.'

A slim curve of smile proclaims Qasem Khan as the victor. He twinkles at Kulsum and then at Hasina. The other five deep pockets congratulate him. 'Mubarak ho!' 'Hail to the Khan!' 'Well done!'

Kulsum Bai then announces that two days later, on Friday, the nath-utarna ceremony will take place.

Once all the other guests leave, Qasem Khan offers a salaam to Hasina and places thirty thousand rupees in her hands. Then, as recognition of her services, he presses two thousand rupees into Kulsum's hand.

Kulsum melts in happiness. 'Shukriya, Khan Saheb!' she chirps as he takes leave of them.

'Seems all right,' Kulsum whispers to Hasina. 'Not too old. Quite manly too!'

Hasina nods with a smile. 'Yes, dear,' she whispers back. 'Praise be to Allah!'

That evening there was a concert for a couple of hours. Almost every known baiji was there: Gulshan Bai, Roshan Bai, Rattan Bai, Munni Bai, Nadira Bai and Kesar Bai. They sat in a circle around a bejewelled, sandalwood-paste-adorned Gulab Banu. Of course Hasina Bai and Kulsum Bai were there too. A veritable bazaar of beauty, it was. The musicians were also well turned out.

The first to take the floor was the twenty-seven-year-old beauty Kesar Bai. '*Saawariya thaharo Jamuna ke teer,* (Wait on the banks of the Jamuna, my beloved)'—Kesar Bai sang the plea of gopinis, and Uday's sarangi echoed the emotion. Jhanu Mallick's fingers rushed from one end of the harmonium to the other like a herd of fawns, pleading to Shyam Rai, 'Come, wait on the banks of Yamuna...'

Then twenty-two-year-old charmer Meher Bai danced as she sang, '*Kuhoo koyaliya kook rahi ban mein...*' Uday Moinuddin's sarangi, too, sang—'A cuckoo calls "coohoo kuhu" in the forest'. The words made Hasina's twenty-four-year-old handmaiden, Rabiya, devour Moinuddin with her eyes.

Naseer Khan's tabla too was relentlessly belting 'coo-hoo'. As soon as Meher Bai stopped, the propitious ceremony started. Gulab would be adorned with a nath. From a small silver box, Hasina took out an antique nose ring of pure gold, studded with a 1.5-carat diamond that was dazzling with its brilliance.

Every visiting baiji's eyes reflected the brilliance of the diamond. They cried out in a chorus, 'Oh my god, what a stunning nath!'

Twenty-eight-year-old Munni Bai nudged Nadira Bai, who

was perhaps thirty, with her elbow. 'So Nadira, want to go for another nath?'

Nadira tickled Munni under her chin. 'If you do, so will I!'

Everyone twittered and fell on each other, giggling.

It flashed through Hasina's mind that some seventeen years ago she had worn this very nose ring, and that rugged man, Gulab's progenitor…

'Come on then! Put on the nath on the bride,' Kulsum's voice cut into her thoughts.

So, in the name of Allah, Nadira Bai affectionately held Gulab Banu's face in her hands and with great care put on the nath.

'Wah! She's looking too beautiful!' Kulsum exclaimed. Gulab shyly giggled and buried her face in her hands. Hasina walked up to her daughter and kissed her forehead. The elders present blessed her while Rattan Bai and Munni Bai joined in singing the Kafi thumri: '*Shyam ki muraliya sakhi, Baj rahi ban mein* (Hark! There in the forest he plays his magic flute.)'

Rabiya could hear the flute of the Dark Cowherd in Uday Moinuddin's sarangi and could see the Divine Lover in him. She put a hand on her breasts, trying to calm the desire churning in her heart. Yes, Shyam's flute was casting its charm…

Hasina could not drift into sleep today, so she was reading a book. She took off the danglers from her ears, then the brassiere that held her curvaceous breasts in place. They were still firm and were far from drooping, she thought to herself as she stared at the semi-nude Hasina in the full-size mirror. Once in a while, she'd make love with some tycoon but she would not feel sated or fulfilled. She had had three nikahs so far. These agreements were all three-month contracts that would end on the ninetieth day. A man had to pay for a nikah, but not as much as he would in a nilaam that auctioned a woman's virginity. Hasina would demand two thousand for each of the three months.

A baiji must earn using her beauty, her youth, her skill in dance or her talent in singing. She has to secure her old age. Yes, they have offspring, but they pray to Allah for a girl child as only a daughter can keep the tradition of a nautch girl alive. They are disappointed if a male child comes along. Most of their sons grow up to be procurers, and pimp for their mothers too. Praise be to Allah, Hasina has just one child, Gulab, and she is beautiful and talented. May Allah's blessings continue to shower upon her!

Who had sired Gulab Banu?

You need to travel sixteen to seventeen years back in time. That was when Hasina was relieved of her nath by a thirty-year-old man. The lean, handsome, fair-skinned hero was Pratap Singh.

'Hasina! Meri jaan, my life!' His endearments continue to ring in her ear.

She donned a thin cotton kameez and sat down on her bed. Pratap had been on her mind all day long.

Hasina is aware of her lineage; she's not some common nautch girl.

In the middle ages, the Nawabs who followed the Mughals would engage skilled dancing girls for their entertainment. In mid-18th century, once the sun set on the Emperor and the Nawabs, this segment of society had to resort to entertaining the barons and the big guns. That is when the word 'baiji' or courtesan became a familiar one in Bengali society. It had a whiff of forbidden pleasure, and therefore was irresistible. These ladies banked on their ability to attract numerous men to make money.

Naturally they came in contact with countless persons, especially in their youth. This created a new echelon in society in which the women adapted their age-old traditions to suit their new circumstances and lifestyle. As marriage is an indispensable part of any society, the tawaifs created a form of marriage that came to be recognized as nath-utarna.

The man who would do the honours would be a husband for three months, at most; after that he would go his way.

This, in effect, marked the debut of a baiji. Then, if love came her way, she would love. She would even enter into relationships for the sheer demands of the body but this, too, would not last. Some secretly got married. But because it curbed their freedom to pursue their profession and affected their livelihood, they altered the accepted concept of marriage and crafted one of their own. By God's will they are in this profession, they argued, so they must accept that they cannot marry like you and I. Only if they give birth to a girl, and if she grows up to be an enchanting courtesan, can they breathe easy for some more years. Allah please shape Gulab Banu into an enchantress!

Hasina remembers the consort who was the protagonist of her nath-utarna: Pratap Singh. Such a charmer he was! There was passion in his love-making, it swept her off her feet and flooded her senses. Pratap, Pratap, where did you disappear after mere two months? Pratap, O Pratap!

What was that sound? Hasina peeped through the door to the small adjacent room. No, Rabiya has gone to sleep. So, what's that sound? Whose footsteps?

Swiftly she opened her door and stepped on to the veranda. The narrow corridor led to the mujra room. Standing there she noticed that the door leading up to the rooftop was ajar.

But Hanif was fast asleep at the bottom of the stairs. So, did someone go upstairs? Who could it be? Gulab? No, the door to her room was shut.

Hasina tiptoed upstairs. It's a moon-bathed night. Sleep had cast its spell over the neighbourhood, and standing still in the midst of the roof, staring at the moon, was Uday Moinuddin.

'Uday!'

Startled, Uday turned around. 'Bai Saheba!'

'Why are you here at the dead of night?'

'Pardon me,' Uday sounded apologetic. 'It won't happen again, Bai.'

'I'm not forbidding that, Uday,' Hasina hastily replied. 'All I'm asking is, why are you here in the middle of the night?'

Uday looked at Hasina and smiled, 'To admire the moon, Bai!'

'To admire the moon?' Hasina was taken aback. 'Because the moon is your Mama?' she teased him and broke into a giggle.

'Yes, we always speak of moon as Chanda Mama but my attraction is for a different reason.'

'What is that reason?' Hasina was curious.

Uday replied, 'My father once mentioned that we, the Moon Dynasty, are descendants of the Moon.'

'Really? Gopi Chacha said that! But why? Is the moon a human being like you and I that it will have descendants and a dynasty?'

Uday did not lose his smile. 'There is logic in what you're saying, Bai, but I didn't argue with Father. I liked the thought very much. I felt proud of my origins. I feel a kinship with the moon and that compels me to come and stand under the night sky. The moon isn't quite visible from my room downstairs...'

Hasina smiled at him. 'It's quite all right. You may come

here to chat with the moon. You can continue gazing, I'll go back to my room.'

'No, Bai, I'll leave now,' Uday said to her. 'I'm sorry I disturbed you.'

He started for the stairway. Hasina called out to him, 'A moment, Uday…'

He turned around. Hasina had an impish smile as she asked, 'Doesn't your ancestor, the moon, advise you to get married?'

Uday looked into her eyes and replied, 'No Bai, not yet.'

'If it does?'

'I don't think it will…'

'Why?'

'The moon knows my mind.'

After he had spoken, Uday hung his head.

Hasina softly responded, 'Now go back to bed, Uday.'

'Yes, Bai,' he replied as he made for the stairs.

Watching him go, Hasina stood there pondering over what Uday had just said: the moon will not advise him to get married. Does that mean Rabiya has not made a mark on him? Poor Rabiya! She is decent in her appearance, she is in the full flush of youth, and for the past four years she has had eyes only for Uday Moinuddin. She is as crazy about his music as Radha was about Krishna's flute. But this man—is he not made of flesh and blood?

Let go. Forget Rabiya. Let us focus on the moon instead. Uday Moinuddin belongs to the Moon Dynasty! Balderdash! Nothing but trying to mark out a status, a rank in society…

Hasina lifted her face to the moon. Sublime! It must have been the twelfth or thirteenth night of the waxing moon. Not a trace of cloud, the moon was basking in its glory alone. Was the Moon truly beautiful? She remembered what Pratap would say: 'Hasina, you are beautiful like the moon… The full moon is all I can think of when I look at you…' Pratap, Pratap! Where art thou?

II

Hasina Baiji's house is at one end of Chitpore. A two-storey building on a street off the main road. Hasina, Gulab Banu, Rabiya, the other members of the family and their attendants live on the upper floor. The concert hall is on the same floor, overshadowing the kitchen and the dining room.

The ground floor has eight rooms. As you enter the building, the stairway is to the right. To the left, on either side of a wide corridor, are three rooms each. The corridor ends in smaller rooms, a bathroom and the kitchen-cum-dining room for the men.

The three rooms facing the main road are Uday Moinuddin's quarters. The rooms on the opposite side of the corridor are of the tabla player Naseer Khan, his wife Noor and their children. Their daughter is married and lives with her in-laws, in Khidderpore. Now the fifteen-year-old son Qamran lives with them and learns the tabla from his guru, his father Naseer.

Uday Moinuddin entered his room. The first room is his drawing room and study. The next one is his bedroom, and the third was for his parents, which after they passed away has been kept just as it used to be. On the eastern wall hangs a patachitra of Radha-Govind; on the western wall a hand-painted image of the Kaaba stone in Holy Mecca. And on the northern wall hangs a portrait of his father Gopichand Uday and mother Hamidan, made by an artist from Delhi. Gopichand is seated in a chair,

Hamidan is standing on his left, her right arm resting on his left shoulder. Not a good portrait but yes, you can see their likeness in it. Below the portrait, on the floor is an agarbatti stand. These days Uday Moinuddin sits in this room, under the portrait, for his practice sessions. After the riyaaz, his dear sarangi rests in this room, for it used to be his father's too.

Uday's father Gopichand was Hindu. His grandfather was Amirchand Uday. 'Uday' is his ancestral surname. They are Rajputs from Rajasthan. But Hamidan was a Mussalman. So how did they come to marry? Here goes the story…

Gopichand Uday was the favourite disciple of Delhi's famed sarangi player Habibullah Khan. With his guru's blessings he too earned a reputation that secured him a place as the chief sarangi player in Hasina's maternal grandmother, Binno Bai's team. All kinds of instruments are played when a baiji dances: harmonium, tanpura, sitar, tabla—but the most important one in this chorus is the sarangi. This sarangi is what leads a dance to the peak of melody and mesmerizes the hearts and brings alive all the senses of the patrons.

Gopichand was twenty-eight years old at the time. And Binno Bai was sheltering her orphaned niece, Hamidan. She did this with the good intention of saving the twenty-year-old from the clutches of a wicked uncle. Hamidan was not exactly pretty but, without doubt, she had a natural appeal. She was neither a singer nor was she good at dancing but she loved to read. Once she got the protection of her paternal aunt, she fell in love with her bua's sarangi player. Not because of his expertise at the string instrument but because of his values. The amazing thing about this love story was that it transcended social barriers and religion.

About six months later Gopichand came to Binno Bai and

spoke with his eyes fixed on the floor, 'Bai Saheba, I have come to bid goodbye.'

Binno Bai was surprised. 'Why Gopichand? Are you unhappy playing for me? Has anyone humiliated you in any way? Do you want in some ways? Or has some other baiji offered you more by way of salary?'

Gopichand shook his head, hesitated for a little, then said, 'Bai Saheba, I have erred. I made a mistake by falling in love with your niece. Hamidan too reciprocates the sentiment. But this might reflect adversely on your reputation. Before it does, it would be better for me to leave.'

Binno Bai looked at Gopichand with a newfound respect. 'Does Hamidan know about this decision you've made?' she asked.

'No, Bai. That would make it more difficult for me to leave. But more important than love is my fidelity to you.'

Binno Bai watched him for some seconds. Then she said, 'Give me a day's time, Gopichand.'

'As you wish, Bai Saheba.'

That afternoon she summoned Hamidan and asked her point blank, 'Are you in love with Gopichand?'

'Yes, bua,' she replied, resting her head in her aunt's lap.

'But he is a Hindu!'

'I can't live without his love, bua!' she whispered.

'Out of respect for me, he wants to leave the team.'

'Bua can't you respect this love of ours?'

Binno Bai thought for a while before speaking. 'Ask Gopichand to convert to Islam.'

'Is that really necessary, bua?' Hamidan asked, lifting her head from her aunt's lap. 'Are human beings not the children of the same Divine Being? Besides, this world of baijis is also a fusion of the two faiths. Don't you, a Muslim, sing of the love and passion of the Hindu deities Radha and Krishna? And that pleases the raees and tycoons of both the faiths. They fall under the spell and nod their heads in appreciation and break into wah-wahs. Am I not right, bua?'

Binno was almost convinced.

'And what if Gopichand doesn't convert to Islam? I will remain a Muslim,' Hamidan continued to speak. 'Such things have happened before. Didn't Shahenshah Akbar marry a Hindu princess? Did Rajput Jodhabai ever convert to Islam?'

'All right then,' Binno Bai acquiesced. 'I have heard you and I have learnt from you. Now, leave me alone. I need to think.'

Hamidan left the room.

Next day Binno Bai summoned Gopichand. 'Don't leave me, Gopichand. Make Hamidan your wife and stay on with us. In our world, there is no conflict between Hindus and Muslims.'

That is what happened.

On an auspicious day as per the Hindu calendar Gopichand and Hamidan went to a Shiva temple and exchanged garlands. Gopichand applied a pinch of sindoor on the parting of Hamidan's hair. Binno Bai watched from a distance. The next Friday they visited a masjid, rested their heads on the steps and prayed, 'Kindly accept us as husband and wife.' This time, too, Binno Bai witnessed it from a distance. That night in his flower-adorned bedroom Gopichand and Hamidan consummated their union. There was great rejoicing all around. Binno Bai's instrumentalists started singing a happy song set in raga Deepchandi: '*Paani bharane naa jaiyo, nazariya lagi jai*... (Do not go to the Jamuna to fetch water, O maiden! You'll attract Krishna's attention...)'

Then one day Hamidan presented Gopichand with a son.

His face had a likeness to both his parents. But what should he be named?

Hamidan pleaded that there should be a bit of 'Islam' in the name. Gopichand smiled. 'It's a custom to name the child after the father, Hami dear!' However, to honour her, he decided to name his son 'Uday', in order to carry forward his family name, and 'Moinuddin' to respect his mother's wish. Thus their son came to be called Uday Moinuddin.

When Uday was about five years old, Binno Bai's daughter Phiroza gave birth to a girl. This child was named Hasina. A certain nawabzada Barkat Ali was the sire.

The very next year Binno Bai passed away. Phiroza suffered a setback. Her childhood friend Amina Bai, who was much in demand in Calcutta at the time, was in Delhi to attend a wedding. When the two friends met, she pleaded with Phiroza to find a place in Calcutta. The city had come to be recognized as a haven for baijis.

After much consideration, Phiroza decided to take the risk. By the grace of Allah, her fame had spread through the Babudom within six months, and she had become a name to be reckoned with. She had come down with her full team and that included Gopichand. Soon Hamidan was Phiroza's cousin, friend, philosopher and attendant—all rolled into one.

The days rolled by. Since his childhood Uday Moinuddin was being trained on the sarangi by his father. When he turned eighteen he sat next to his father and played for Phiroza Bai's concerts. The seths and babus who heard him play praised him, 'Wah! The son of an ustad all right! An ustad in his youth… Well done!'

Meanwhile Hasina too was growing up. The bonny child

was blossoming into an irresistible beauty who was as alluring a singer as she was a seductive dancer.

Even as a child Hasina was fond of jalebis. But Phiroza was not in favour of indulging this love for sweets. So once in a while Hasina would look for Uday, disrespectfully address him with the informal 'tui', and say, 'Hey! Go get four crisp jalebis from Enayet Mithaiwala. Here's an anna!'

Uday would get it for her.

Away from people's gaze, before she bit into the sweets, she would offer one to Uday. 'Here, have one…'

'No, I'm not fond of jalebi.'

Hasina would be confounded. 'Don't like jalebi? What's with you? You're a… a…' she would bite into a jalebi and then complete the sentence, 'You're an ass!'

One day Phiroza took her aside and told Hasina, 'Moinuddin is senior to you, he's your elder cousin, you should address him more respectfully.'

'No Maa, whenever I speak with him, "tui" is what comes naturally—' Hasina trotted off.

Phiroza smiled indulgently. Still naïve and playful! She will improve her ways by and by.

Finally it was time for Hasina's nath-utarna.

The atmosphere in this house was festive for days. All of a sudden Hasina noticed that Uday was watching her fixedly, from a distance. She knitted her brows, then went up to him and rudely asked, 'Why are you devouring me with your eyes, Uday?'

Uday smiled, 'Just thinking about your approaching happiness.'

'Are you unhappy that I'll be happy?'

'Fie! Govind alone knows what's going on in my mind!'

'Govind? Who's that?'

'Govind is Allah Rasul—'

'Get lost, you Hindu!'

Uday smiled as he spoke. 'I'm a Hindu because my father is a Hindu. But at the same time I'm a Mussalman, Hasina, because my mother is a Muslim. I'm Uday Moinuddin, so I know that He who is Allah is also Govind.'

'Keep your preaching to yourself!' Hasina sharply retorted. 'Listen, never ever devour me with your eyes again, understand?'

Uday bowed his head down. 'No, Hasina, I won't ever again.' Without another word he turned around and left.

After her nath-utarna ceremony, when she performed her first mujra, Hasina observed that Gopi Chacha was playing on one side, next to him Jhanu Mallick was playing the harmonium, and then Naseer Khan was on the tabla. Further away sat Uday Moinuddin. Now the father Gopichand would show his mastery over the sarangi, then the son would display his skill with the same instrument. All the musicians were looking at Hasina—save Uday.

Showing off her enticing youth, Hasina sang, '*Bula ke pardes mein chale gaye chhaliya, Aaj yeh raat yauvan masti bhari...* (My paramour sent for me and then left for a far-off land, On this night, young and promising...)'

Her gestures, her expression, her sidelong glances evoked a storm of 'Hai hai!' Babu Gauri Shankar De and all his cohorts raved about her dancing. They took care not to take their eyes off her. They were willing to sacrifice their last breath for her, they said. But Gopi Chacha's son? Why wasn't he lifting his lowered head? Hasina realized why. And as she realized, she chortled even as she danced on.

Devastated by this, the lusty Babus and their hangers-on

broke into fresh bouts of cheering. Now and then they also praised Uday's playing, 'Wah sarangi! Peerless!' But no, Uday would not look up.

The next morning, Hasina urgently sent for Uday. A while later he stood outside her room, head bowed down, and asked, 'Did you send for me Hasina?'

She was sitting on a chair. 'Yes I did. Come in—'

Uday set a foot in her room. 'Sit,' Hasina commanded, 'on that chair.'

Uday did not look at Hasina, his eyes fixed on the floor he said, 'Tell me what you wanted to…'

'Not until you sit down…' Hasina said, rising from her chair.

This compelled Uday to sit down but his gaze was still fixed on the floor.

Hasina walked up to a table, picked up a silver bowl with a silver spoon in it and offered it to Uday. 'Moinuddin, have this.'

Uday looked at the bowl. It held the most loved Bengali sweets, rasgullas. Many of them.

'Why, suddenly, rasgullas?' Uday asked without raising his head.

Hasina spoke softly, 'Forgive me, Moinuddin. Do look at me henceforth when you speak with me. If you have these rasgullas, I'll know you've forgiven me.'

Uday did not lift his head as he said, 'You have one first.'

Hasina pulled out a low stool, put the bowl on it, put one in her mouth, then responded 'H-u-uh-' indicating to Uday that she had partaken of the sweets, and now it was his turn.

Uday picked up a rasgulla and put it in his mouth, then looked into Hasina's eyes and said, 'I have, too.'

Hasina grinned, 'Don't be angry with me for what I say.'

Uday replied, 'I wasn't angry, Hasina Bai, I was only complying with your mandate.'

'Now there's a new mandate.'

Uday smiled. 'Whatever you command! But first, tell me Hasina, why have you suddenly altered your mode of addressing me, from the chatty "tui" to the mannerly "tumi"?'

Hasina spoke in a sombre tone. 'You are elder to me, and I was an imbecile. Maa used to scold me, but I was wilful, adamant. Now I realize it was wrong of me to speak in that manner. Besides, you are the talented son of a talented musician. I ought to be deeply respectful towards you.'

Uday was equally sombre. 'Don't you dare, Hasina! I'll be forced to fix my gaze on the floor once again... Hasina Bai, you are no less talented. It is because you excel in your singing and dancing that our playing becomes so melodious.'

Hasina's eyes glistened at this. 'Have another rasgulla, Moinuddin!'

'I'd rather have a jalebi if you can bring one—'

Hasina broke into a giggle. She replied, 'You'll have one this evening!'

'I'll take your leave now?'

'See you later.'

As he came out of her room, it suddenly struck Uday that every girl transforms into a woman after her marriage. In this case, it was the nath-utarna.

A year later, Hasina became a mother. Her fame spread beyond Calcutta, to Banaras, Delhi and Lucknow too. Connoisseurs came from far and wide to hear her sing and were mesmerized by her naach. Phiroza Bai now scaled down her performance. Only when a high-ranking guest visited them, would she hum a few lines and then leave it to her daughter to bring it to its finale.

The year after Gulab Banu was born, Phiroza Bai passed away. And two years after that Uday's father, Gopichand. Alas!

One day, like on every other morning, he was doing his riyaaz. Uday was yet to wake up. Suddenly, his strings struck an odd note. He cried out in pain, 'Hami- Ha-mi- Bi-Bi-' Hamidan was pouring hot milk for her husband in his well-polished silver glass. She put it down and rushed to his side, 'What's the matter!'

Gopichand put aside his sarangi and put his hand to his chest, 'Pain! Excruciating—oof!'

'What kind of pain?' Hamidan asked as she sat down beside him and massaged his chest.

In reply Gopichand put his head in her lap and lay down. 'Can't breathe—so painful! Ha-mi—pyari...'

'Beta Moin—' Hamidan screamed for her son, 'Moin!'

Uday sprang to his feet. 'What's it, Ma?'

'Your father! Get the hakim! Run!'

Gopichand groped for Hamidan as if he couldn't see. 'Hami—Narayan!' And the next moment he was lying still, next to his sarangi, his head in the lap of his beloved wife. He had left for Heavens.

Holding on to his body, Hamidan sat like she had turned into stone. Hasina came running down. Ajmal Khan, the white-bearded hakim, felt Gopichand's pulse and pronounced, 'He's already with the Lord!'

Hamidan did not cry. She simply kept caressing her husband's face and head. A couple of hours later, when people gathered to take him to the burning ghat, she let go of him. That is when she let out a heart-wrenching cry, 'Why didn't you take me along with you?' And fainted the very next moment.

Uday went to the cremation ground, where he lit his father's pyre.

Hamidan lived for only two more months. She hardly spoke, looked after her son, and would sit staring blankly into nothing. Whenever she could make time, Hasina would go and sit quietly beside her. On one such occasion, Hamidan softly said to her, 'O my ladli, will you sing me that song just once, dear?' And Hasina sang:

Piya bin nahin aawat chaen…
Din nahin chaen, raat nahin nindiya—kaase kahun ab bain re…

(With my beloved gone there's no such thing as peace.
Can't be still during the day, can't sleep a wink at night,
who can I share my thoughts with?)

Utter loneliness, sheer emptiness. One morning, two months after his father's death, Uday woke up to see his mother was still in bed. 'Maa,' he called her, 'time to rise…' No reply. No movement whatsoever. His mother had already set out on a long journey to be united with her favourite sarangi player. Everlasting peace for her!

Days went by. Phiroza Bai, Gopichand, Hamidan all became stories. Everyone kept adding years to their age. And Hasina's lovely daughter Gulab Banu turned into a Basra rose. Two days from now she will be wedded in a nath-utarna ceremony.

Time! Are you a river or an ocean?

The memory of his parents brought tears to Uday's eyes. He splashed some water on his face and poured a drink for himself. Today, he felt like having a drink. A lot was going through his mind.

He thought of the moment on the terrace a while ago. Hasina had said, 'That Moon, your ancestor, doesn't it advise you to marry?'

Uday knows the unasked question: 'Uday, won't you marry Rabiya?'

This girl had come to this household around four years ago from a suburb of Calcutta. To be an attendant for Hasina. At the age of twenty-four. Her marriage had been finalized six years ago but the groom was bitten by a snake and had died. Since then no one had mentioned marriage for her. Her family was not well-off, so she had come to Hasina. Good girl, she is. Hasina has a lot of affection for her. She is keen for Uday to marry her. It would spell a repetition of the Gopichand–Hamidan story. But no, that will not happen, Hasina. That moon in the sky will not tell Uday to marry yet.

Rabiya is genuinely a good soul. Three or four times a day, she would come to Uday on some pretext or the other. 'Moin Saheb, Bai has sent me to serve you tea.'

'Shukriya, Rabiya,' Uday would smile faintly.

She wouldn't leave. She would talk this and that, her eyes fixed on Uday's face, mesmerized. She cannot break herself away. She would leave only after Uday said, 'Rabiya go now, see to what your mistress needs.'

Just the other day, Rabiya came with some hot jalebis. 'Bai sahiba has sent these.'

'Shukriya, Rabiya.'

'Forget the thanks! I'm not the one to get these for you, they've been sent by—'

'I know, Rabiya, but you cared to bring them to me.'

'You speak so well, Saheb!

She stood staring at Uday, enchantment in her eyes.

'Carry on, Rabiya, your mistress might need your service.'

Rabiya did not smile. 'I know what she will need at what time. If I hang around for a while, do you feel distressed?' she sulked.

'Not distressed, Rabiya, but why should you needlessly stand around?'

'I have my reasons.'

'And what would they be?'

'You play the sarangi so well, Moin Saheb! It causes an upheaval inside me. I am overtaken by a happiness tinged with sadness…'

Uday was startled. He looked at Rabiya anew. 'Wah, you put it so well, Rabiya! My music becomes melodious by the grace of Govind, by Allah's blessing.'

Rabiya lowered her voice as she pleaded, 'Would you play a bit for me? I'm eager to hear your music.'

Uday smiled. 'I'll play for you when you perform mujra, Rabiya.'

Rabiya looked at him with stilled eyes. 'In other words, not in my lifetime. Moin Saheb, you play a soulful sarangi but deep down you are a heartless person.'

Promptly she left the room.

Uday Moinuddin sat in silence. He felt somewhat wistful. But he could not help it. One must speak the truth, at times. Rabiya's sapling of hope cannot be allowed to flourish.

A wind of happiness is blowing through the whole house. Hullabaloo, commotion, hoo-ha, to-do, fuss, hurly-burly… Tomorrow is the nath-utarna ceremony. Now, Gulshan Bai is singing in the concert room; next, Roshan Bai will hold the floor.

Unexpectedly they decide to sing a duet. Sometimes, in a trice, the musicians take centre stage. Out of the blue, the women oust the instrument players and themselves play the tanpura, dhol and manjira.

Jaani na maaro pichkari...
O Kanhaiya, araj kari haari—
Gari main doongi tokey, na darungi...
Aisan hai dheet Kanhai—Gari main doongi...

(Do not shower me with the coloured water of your pichkari!
O Kanhaiya, I plead with you...
I will shower abuses if you do! I won't fear to shower you too...
Oh! How adamant you are Krishna!)

In the next room, Kulsum Bai regaled even as she chewed on a paan, while Nadira Bai cheered her on.

Nadiya kinare herayi, aayi kangana!

(O! I lost my bracelet on the banks of the river...)

Elsewhere Uday Moinuddin is playing the sarangi, with Jhanu Mallick, Sagiruddin and Naseer Khan accompanying him. So, Rattan Bai or Munni Bai decide to sing:

Kaise kahoon sharam ki baat...

(How can I recount the shameful feat.)

Listening to the song, Naghma Bai whispered to her friend and peer, Zohra Bai, 'Do you recall the shameless feats of your first night?'

Zohra nodded with a twinkle, 'Vividly!'

Naghma grasped Zohra's hand in hers, 'Tell me! Tell me all!'

Zohra pushed her off as she whispered, 'I will, after you tell me all! Hee-hee...'

From the day of the auction until the night of nath-utarna, no business will be conducted in this establishment. Hence, friends and relatives are frequenting the household, keeping Hasina Bai on her toes.

Gulab Banu's room is overflowing with presents. Gold, silver, jewellery, clothing… Some of her patrons, some valued customers, reputed seths and eminent babus have been stopping by with gifts. They bless Gulab with auspicious silver coins, but they cannot stifle a sigh as their eyes fall on her nath. Pity, they could not claim her virginity for themselves. But why is she looking weary? She is doing everything, fulfilling all her duties, but something seems to be weighing on her mind.

The next morning, Uday was practising on his sarangi when in walked Gulab Banu. Probably fresh out of bed. Straightaway she seated herself on Uday's bed and addressed him, 'Uday Chacha…'

The sarangi stopped. Uday looked at her and spoke with deep affection, 'Yes beti, tell me?'

Gulab confided in him, 'I'm not happy with anything, Chacha.'

'Why Gulab? Who have you fought with?' Uday asked with a fond smile.

'No, Chacha no, no fight—' she shook her head. 'All this crowd, so much noise, even the gifts are getting on my nerves.'

Uday smiled. In order to reassure Gulab, he said, 'Each of these is an inevitable part of every festivity—in particular, of happy occasions like weddings. The routine goes for a toss. Later, you'll find that this very noise and clamour has become a part of your happy memories.'

Gulab again shook her head to say, 'No Chacha, I'm feeling hunted. I just don't like anything.'

She stood up and went out of the room. 'Gulab beta! Gulabo listen—'

But Gulab did not stop to listen, she did not return to his room. Uday felt compassion for Gulab. She was different from girls her age. More sensitive. Mercurial. Besides, this nath-utarna signified the end of one chapter of life and the start of a new one. Poor child!

All the sounds were percolating down. Laughter. Footsteps. Snatches of songs. The dancers' footwork. Gradually each sound started growing in volume and was joined in by various scents. The fragrance of ittar, flowers and garlands. The smell of kebabs and biryani. Aah! It was the night of nath-utarna—the curtain call of an adolescent's virginity.

Out of the blue, Hasina appeared in front of Uday. Leaving a bunch of baijis to entertain themselves, she had come with a pile of jalebis on a silver platter!

'Uday Moinuddin,' her voice resonated above the festivity in the air, 'have some jalebis.'

Uday broke into laughter. 'You've gone mad, Hasina Bai. So many jalebis!'

'Go on! Finish them all. It's a happy day for us. My daughter will take off on a new track of life…'

'Right you are! Come, give them to me, give them to me, I'll have them all.' Hasina giggled like a little girl. 'As a child I could not quite be happy until you secretly got me jalebis. To pay back for that rare happiness, I'll treat you to jalebis as long as I live.'

'What a lovely thought, Hasina Bai!' Uday's voice was drenched in emotion.

Hasina turned to look at Uday, hesitated for a moment and then said, 'Uday, can I say something to you? You could think of it as an appeal.'

'Tell me, Hasina.'

'Rabiya is a very good girl, why don't you marry her?'

Uday was quiet for a few seconds. Then he smiled. He looked squarely at Hasina and said, 'I admit that Rabiya is indeed a very good girl. But Bai, I will not marry her.'

'Why, Uday?' Hasina paused before going on, 'Don't mind my asking you, but do you love someone else?'

Uday replied in a calm voice, 'Yes, Bai Saheba, I love someone else. My sarangi.'

Hasina laughed out in disbelief. Then she made to go. 'Bye Uday, the guests are arriving.'

As she departed, Hasina thought to herself, 'Uday is so cold-blooded!' And to think that ten years ago this very man took on, all by himself, ten professional lathiyals sent by the wealthy cloth merchant, Haider Ali. The way he fought the goons that day—who would have believed that Uday was a sarangi player?

Haider Ali must have been forty years old then and Hasina twenty-five. She was attracted to the handsome, hardy Haider. They had contracted a three-month nikah. But after the initial exhilaration, Hasina became conscious of the fact that Haider was a sadist. Then she would pretend illness to bide by the three months of nikah. But Haider Ali was obdurate and unrelenting. Hasina rebelled. She ordered her bodyguards to ensure that Haider was not allowed to enter the house. Going by the contract, there were ten more days to go. But Hasina was ridden with countless marks of abuse all over her body. So her bodyguards stopped Haider Ali from seeing her. He had to go back.

Uday counselled Hasina Bai to approach the Police Commissioner's wife and plead for the Commissioner's intervention. He accompanied her along with her bodyguards to Commissioner Harold's house. With great difficulty, Hasina secured permission to meet the commissioner's wife. She narrated her plight in detail, and revealed the many sores and marks of abuse on her body to bear her out, and convinced the lady. But no sooner had she returned home when ten of Haider's hoodlums raided them. While a maidservant was dispatched to the nearest police station to get help, it was Uday's unabated courage that saved the day with a single lathi and a handful of chowkidars. By the time four rifle-carrying constables arrived on the scene, the hoodlums had overpowered Uday and were dragging Hasina out of the house.

Hasina was saved. Harold Saheb got Haider Ali arrested and imprisoned for a couple of days, to teach him a lesson. Hasina had to face no other problem, ever, neither from Haider nor any other pervert. All thanks to Uday.

Still, Hasina wondered: Is Uday a man of flesh and blood? Is he not a full-bodied man? Why else would he reject Rabiya? Well, let things play out...

III

A little while later, the rituals started. Almost all in the likeness of a Hindu wedding.

Since the morning dawned, Gulab had had nothing but a bowl of milk. Around ten in the morning, Gulshan Bai, Roshan Bai, Meher Bai, Kesar Bai and Nadira Bai smeared her with turmeric. Gulab turned golden. During this haldi ceremony they sang, '*Aao sakhi sringar karein, Piya milan aaj ratiya*... (Come dear friend, let's adorn you. It's the night of union with your beloved.)'

The rest of the day, too, there was singing and teasing. From time to time, Gulab Banu was served a sherbet or a cool drink of scented water. Then, when the sun set in the west, Gulab was decked up like a bride. By now all the guests, mostly baijis, had showed up. In all there must have been some twenty-five ladies. In addition there were about ten men and of course the musicians, the servants, the attendants, the pimps…

Long before sundown the entrance to the building was done up with festive flowers and auspicious deodar leaves. Every floor glittered with rows and rows of tiny bulbs that compelled the glow of daylight to return after dusk. And that is when Uday Moinuddin, Jhanu Mallick, Naseer Khan and Sagiruddin started playing on their instruments. Then, when darkness descended on the roads and residences that make Calcutta, Qasem Khan arrived on a carriage drawn by two powerful horses. Attired in fancy clothes, he donned a string of pearls around his neck and flashed diamonds on four fingers of his right hand. He had two bodyguards with him. An attendant followed with a box on his head carrying Qasem Khan's clothes, another carried four-five large bouquets of rose.

He was welcomed on the second floor by Hasina Bai. 'Tashreef laiye…'

Kulsum led him by his hand to his seat. At once Meher Bai and Kesar Bai broke into a song: '*Dulha aaya re, piya aaya re, Khushi se dulhaniya ka dil dola re* (Here comes the groom, the beloved himself, He sets aflutter the heart of the bride.)'

But, covered in jewellery and fragrant flowers though she was, the nath-adorned bride was far from happy. Gulab Banu's heart was in the grip of an unknown fear. To assuage her fears her friends Rehana and Ayesha, who had had their nath-utarna a year before her, recounted their experiences all through the afternoon, and to the minutest detail, with the background score of giggles and chuckles and chortles. Still they could not calm her.

A while later Kulsum, Hasina, Nadira and Kesar brought Gulab Banu to Qasem Khan. A smile was playing on his lips.

'Tasleem!' Gulab curtsied. He responded with a respectful bow of his head.

'The man looks awesome!' the ladies whispered to one another. Kulsum made the duo stand next to each other. Then she addressed a middle-aged Muslim gentleman seated at a distance, 'Meer Saheb, shall we get things going?'

Meer Saheb smiled as he rose and walked up to the couple. 'Salaam!' Qasem Khan greeted him. Gulab said, 'Tasleem!'

Kulsum Bai fetched two fragrant garlands of jasmine on a shining silver platter. Meer Saheb picked them up and handed one each to the bride and the groom. Then in a singsong voice, he recited the Arabic words and told Qasem and Gulab, 'Put these garlands around each other...'

Accordingly, Qasem put the garland around Gulab. Her hands were shivering as she lifted the garland. She was much shorter. Smiling, Qasem bent forward, and Gulab could put her garland around him. All the ladies twittered.

Meer Saheb took Gulab's left hand and placed it in Qasem's right hand. 'May Khuda shower you with His peace and happiness! Inshallah.'

'Inshallah! May His Grace be showered on you!' the assembled guests echoed.

Qasem Khan saluted Meer Saheb. Gulab too did a bandagi. He dipped his hand into the pocket of his sherwani and took out 500 rupees. Holding it in the palm of both his hands he offered it to Meer Saheb, 'Please oblige by accepting this, huzoor!'

A smiling Meer Saheb picked up the notes and blessed them, 'May Merciful Khuda grant you happiness and prosperity.'

As if on cue, Uday Moinuddin's sarangi started to sing. Naseer Khan's tabla started galloping like a happy horse. And Jhanu Mallick's finger started showing off on the reeds of the harmonium.

All the bais retired Qasem and Gulab to their room for the wedding night. The bed had been decorated with flowers, and their fragrance had fused with that of an expensive agarbatti. Roshanara Bai start singing: '*Balam teri kasam, ghoonghat na utaaro, Mujhe sharm jo lage… Aur dil jo dhadke, mujhe tumhi samharo…* (Oh my cherished! Do not lift the veil off my face. I swear upon you. I am embarrassed… And if my heart flutters uncontrollably, you will have to tend to me—)'

Hee-hee-hee. Ha-ha.

But Gulab could not bring herself to join in the laughter. There was trepidation, a foreboding that just would not let her be.

Dinner was over. But the merriment went on.

When the clock in the not-so-distant police station sounded twelve gongs, Kulsum Bai entered the nuptial room and commanded, 'Girls, let the bride and the groom gather their breath now. Come on, get up and file out of the room… it's past midnight!'

Hee-hee-hee. Ha-ha. With joyous exchanges, the Bais exited the room. Kulsum Bai looked at Qasem and spoke in a serious tone, 'Shut the door, Janab.'

'Ji, Bai Saheba.'

Qasem shut the door and turned towards Gulab. She lowered her eyes. The inquietude had only grown in the meantime.

It was another memorable day in Hasina's life. With the nath-utarna this night, the most precious treasure of her life, her daughter Gulab Banu would embark on a new chapter of life, as a professional baiji.

Gulab's father Pratap Singh was a moneybag from Bihar. Her own progenitor, Mohammad Ali, was a nawabzada from Uttar Pradcsh. Once or twice she had heard about him from Phiroza Bai. She recalled him being a handsome, poet-like person. Soft-spoken and mild-mannered. He had taken her mother's virginity but she seldom spoke of him. Unlike her, Hasina treasured the memory of Pratap Singh. He knew how to win hearts with mere words. He was skilled at playing on the heart-strings of women. Simultaneously she was initiated into the multifarious delights of sex by this thirty-something man who was as handsome as a sculpture.

Alas! Where did the person disappear? He spent only about six weeks with her after the nath-utarna. After some months, in desperation she had requested Uday Moinuddin to go in search of him. Why, and where had the man vanished?

Uday made many inquiries in several places, and followed up the search by visiting some places. Finally he got the news: Pratap Singh was the son of an extremely wealthy father who had two wives. When Pratap's mother passed away, he came with a pot of money to 'have fun' in Delhi. That is where he happened to see Hasina, and became the protagonist of her nath-utarna. But a few weeks later he returned to Bihar because he learnt that under the influence of his stepmother, his father had decided to disown him and was on the verge of willing away his entire property in favour of the son from his second marriage. Beyond that no one could tell Uday much.

Days after Pratap's disappearance, Hasina showed signs of pregnancy. Born out of that was Gulab Banu, Hasina's future inheritor. Year after year has gone by since, but Pratap has not faded from her heart. That tall, robust physique and manly beauty named Pratap.

Qasem Khan drew out a small jewellery box from the pocket of his kurta. He opened the box and placed it in front of Gulab Banu. 'Take a look. How's this?'

Gulab looked. And was dazzled by the mountain of light from the box. A diamond ring.

'Beautiful,' she softly replied. Softly, because she was well aware that at this moment, following custom, some bais were right outside the room, with their ears glued to the door. They will eavesdrop on the exchange between her and Khan. Their talking, their footsteps, and every other sound will be dissected by the ladies. What a distasteful custom!

Qasem spoke in a voice to match her softness, 'Not more beautiful than you. No diamond or pearl can be prettier than you. Let me see you right hand—'

'Why?' Gulab was curious.

Qasem smiled in mischief as he replied, 'Want to bite you.'

That compelled Gulab to smile. Although the trepidation did not leave her, she lifted her right hand.

An impressive ruby was flashing red on the ring finger of her hand. Qasem put the diamond ring on her little finger and said, 'This piece of diamond is fortunate to be on the finger of my rose.' Saying that, he bent slightly forward and lightly kissed her hand. Still, his feverish breath spread the message of fear in every drop of blood coursing through Gulab's body. Cautiously she withdrew her hand.

The move did not go unnoticed by Qasem. He smiled at

her. 'I believe you can play chess. Let's play a few moves.' He picked up the chessboard from a corner of the room, spread it on the bed, arrayed the pieces in their opening positions and sat down to face Gulab.

She was watching him in a detached manner. Now she spoke up. 'I don't like to play chess all the time—'

Qasem grinned. 'Why not play for a short while? Then we can go on to other games.'

Gulab Banu frowned. 'What does that mean?'

Qasem looked squarely at Gulab, then said jokingly, 'Everything doesn't need to have a meaning, Gulab Banu… Wait—'

Qasem rose from the bed and walked up to the silver water-jug. Next to it were two wine goblets. Resting close to that was his leather suitcase. He opened it to bring out a bottle of whisky. He poured some in the two goblets, added a little water, placed it on a handsome silver tray, rested it next to the chessboard and sat down on the bed. A strong scent of intoxicant blended in with the fragrance of attar and flowers.

Lifting one goblet, he offered it to Gulab. 'Here Bibi, have a drink.'

This alarmed Gulab Banu. 'Alcohol!'

Qasem lowered his voice another octave. 'This is a medicine, it will calm your fears.'

'Fears?' Gulab was ruffled.

'Yes. Have a sip. You'll enjoy playing chess then. Go on.'

'N-n-n-no,' Gulab drew back from him.

Qasem held Gulab's hand with his left hand and said, 'I swear by you, Bibijaan. Have you never had even a sip of alcohol? Hasn't your mother offered it to you since you grew up?'

Gulab did not utter a word. But the words 'calm your fear' started taking effect. Why not try if it really does? She noticed that there was less alcohol in the glass offered to her by the burly hulk who was to take off her nose ring.

Without notice she grabbed the goblet and sipped at it. Yes, this year a couple of times her mother did offer her sips from her glass.

Qasem smiled. He took a large sip from his glass and put it down. 'Come, let's play chess. You start. Move the Queen.'

The whisky was coursing through her veins, spreading its warmth through her body. It felt good. Gulab moved the white queen.

The game was in progress.

Gulab's lips curved in a smiled. Qasem was cornered. Gulab was enjoying the moment. She took another sip of her glass. Yes, the flutter in her heart was tamed.

Hasina felt like a drink. After the tumult of these last few days she was drained. She poured a stiff drink in a glass and sipped. There was a hint of smile on her lips. Naghma and Zohra are eavesdropping outside Gulab's bedroom. Curiosity is natural in these green years, but Roshan Bai and Nadira are also there, ears glued to the door.

Her own nath-utarna played out before her eyes. Pratap had said, 'Hasina, your face puts the moon to shame. Let me have a good look.' He had bent forward, intently gazing at her face, and then suddenly kissed her. A long and breathtaking kiss, it had brought the heavens to her! Then he held her in his strong arms and she had melted into him! Pratap, oh Pratap.

Uday's mellifluous sarangi wound its way into her solitude.

He was playing as decided, and following custom, he was to play for at least an hour. To pour music into the union of Gulab and Qasem Khan. How musical his playing is! Aaha! Then she broke into a cynical smile. What will his ancestor, the moon, tell him tonight?

The disquiet was almost gone. And Uday Chacha's sarangi was casting a spell in the air. Aaha! How mellifluous his playing is! Gulab took one more sip of her drink. The palpable warmth of wellness made her happy.

Qasem Khan was losing to her on the chess board. Gulab was smiling.

Qasem observed that smile, deciphered its meaning, and was entertained. Now, after much thought, and in full knowledge of the consequence, he played a wrong move.

It made Gulab thoughtful. Her mind on the knights and horses, she lifted her glass to her lips. Then she moved a piece and declared, 'You are checkmated, Janab!'

She flashed him the smile of a victor.

'Really?' Qasem looked at the pieces on the board and pretended as if he was trying his level best to come out of the corner. Then, regret in his voice, he said, 'I seem to have been irrevocably checkmated! You have won.' Then he added, 'I admire your intelligence!' He took a long sip of his drink. 'Great, Gulab Banu! Well done.'

Gulab was mighty pleased. She too sipped on her glass and looked at Qasem Khan. Now she thought to herself, 'This man is brawny and personable.'

Qasem gazed at her. 'Gulab, you have been rightly named. You are indeed as beautiful as a rose.' Gulab shyly lowered her head.

Qasem carried on, 'That's not all. You also have the glow of the full moon.'

At this, Gulab lifted her head and bestowed him with an enticing smile. At once Qasem said, 'Let me see the black mole on the left of your upper lip! Wow!' And before she could realize it, he lowered his face and pressed his lips on her rosy lips.

Gulab Banu could barely utter an inaudible 'N-n-nnno!' Soon that word was silenced, and she did not withdraw her lips.

Away from the scene, Uday's sarangi was playing an intoxicating thumri in Raga Desh, the ever popular, '*Saiyan mosey kaahe karat thithori…* (Why, my dearest, are you teasing me?)' And on the other side of the door, a suppressed giggle blended into the music of the sarangi.

Uday kept playing. And he kept praying. May this chapter of Gulab Banu's life be filled with happiness, Oh Allah! Oh Govind!

After almost two hours of playing Uday put his sarangi to rest and went back to his room. Everyone seemed to have fallen asleep, with a few exceptions.

His door was merely shut, not locked. There was no need to while he was at home. The house was well guarded at all hours by security men.

He went in and put the latch in place. A sleepy lantern was diffusing the darkness in the room; he brightened it a bit and entered his bedroom. He was stunned: on a durrie spread out on the floor next to his bed, resting her head on his pillow was Rabiya. She was beautifully attired and looking an eyeful. Her fulsome breasts were loudly announcing their presence in her life. And, on her nose shone a blood-red ruby nath.

With the sarangi still in his hand, he stood riveted, looking at Rabiya. Was she really sleeping?

He put the sarangi in its place and softly called out, 'Rabiya!'

There was no response from her. He thought for a while, then knelt near her, rested his right hand on her head and shook her, 'Rabiya!'

This time Rabiya opened her eyes, as though she had come out of a slumber. For a few seconds she simply looked at him, then slowly she sat up, and smiled. 'Moin Saheb, there was too much chaos upstairs, that's why I had come down here. I was too sleepy!'

'Now things have quietened. You can go back to rest upstairs. It's late at night.'

Uday stood up. At this moment Rabiya was actually looking very attractive.

Rabiya also stood up, and covered her breasts with her odhni. Then she looked at Uday with a strange light in her eyes. With a meaningful smile on her lips she murmured, 'Moin Saheb, I have also put on a nath today…'

'Yes, I can see that.'

Rabiya went on in that same sotto voce, 'Kindly do me the honour of taking it off. I want to be your minion for life!' She lowered her head.

Uday Moinuddin could not break his silence. He looked on at Rabiya, head lowered, nath shining on her nose. Then, in a soft voice he addressed her, 'Rabiya, girls like you are few and rare on this earth. But I plead with you, be kind enough not to ask for me.'

Silence thickened in the room.

Rabiya did not move. She stood as before, her eyes fixed on the ground.

Uday was agonized. 'I beg of you Rabiya—' He knelt at her

feet and spoke on, 'don't torment yourself by any thought of me. I am certain Allah will shortly bring us a true match for you.' Then, he folded his hands and said in an impassioned voice, 'You be my sister, Rabiya!'

Now Rabiya lifted her eyes to Uday. Her lips quivered with unstated emotion. Tears welled up in her eyes and flowed down her cheeks.

Desolate, Uday could only say, 'Rabiya!'

She said nothing; only walked up to the door in a few quick steps, opened it, checked both sides of the corridor and left.

Uday kept sitting on his knees. There was a tumult in his heart at the thought of what Rabiya was going through. But, no, he could not bring her into his life simply to be kind.

Hey Govind, oh Allah, please be Rabiya's protector!

Next day.

The daily routine was yet to kick in; consequence of the indiscipline that is very much a part of any celebration. Late nights, late mornings.

Over breakfast Naghma and Zohra shared with other bais the salacious details of their eavesdropping on the previous night.

At around 9:30 a.m. Gulab Banu showed up in her mother's room.

Hasina smiled, then spread out her arms to fold her in an embrace. Gulab hugged her tight. 'All is good?' Hasina murmured.

Gulab laughed, hid her face in her mother's bosom, and held up her right hand for her mother. Hasina looked at the ring with admiration. Expensive, the diamond. 'Have a quick bath and go back to Khan Saheb,' she advised her daughter.

'I am sleepy, Amma. Let me sleep for a while,' Gulab beseeched.

'Fine, then, go sleep off for half an hour.'

Gulab spread herself out on her mother's bed. Hasina came away from her room and decided to look up Qasem Khan.

The door to Gulab's bedroom was half ajar. Peeping through it she could see Qasem sprawled out on the bed. He was lying on his left, his uncovered back to the door. Her eyes fell on the upper right corner of the fair-bodied Khan's back. There, she noticed, was a cut-mark about three-inches wide. Hasina studied the scar for a while, then moved away.

Around 11 a.m., Qasem Khan hurriedly left with his men, to attend to some important business. An urgent matter that had cropped up demanded his personal intervention. But, he assured Gulab Banu, he would certainly be back before ten at night.

Gulab was no longer scared. So, before departing, when Qasem pulled her to his chest, she happily became his plaything.

In the evening, Hasina suddenly appeared in Uday's room. He was reading a Hindi novel. He rose to his feet to welcome her. 'Come, Bai Saheba.' Then he smiled and added, 'By God's grace, everything has gone off well.'

Hasina nodded in assent. 'Yes, Uday, there's no end to Lord's grace. Another four-five days and we can start our mujras. Gulab can also join in after a few days. The brokers already have a handful of proposals.'

'All by the grace of Govind!'

Hasina knitted her brow at this. 'But Govind didn't show mercy to Rabiya. A short while ago she left. She doesn't want to serve here any longer. Not even if she is paid more. She tearfully entreated me to let her go. "I won't live if I stay here," is what she said at parting. So I had to bid her goodbye.'

As soon as she had spoken, Hasina walked out of his room.

Uday realized why she had conveyed this news to him. Indirectly, she denounced him for Rabiya's departure. But he was helpless. You cannot compel your heart to love or not to love. Still, the thought of Rabiya made him sorrowful.

IV

Qasem Khan is now a familiar figure in this house. Indeed, a well-loved member of the household. Gulab Banu's husband, the one who has done the honour of nath-utarna. He now has free entry through the doors.

Every evening he drives in, in his two-horse carriage. He is head over heels about his latest addiction, Gulab Banu. He will not let her do any mujra yet. He alone comes into the concert hall, listens to her singing, and watches her dance. He pays exactly what the brokers are offering for an open recital. At the end of the evening's performance he proceeds to Gulab's room. There, he first indulges in his long-time inebriant, then his newfound intoxication. And the days that find other babus or seths holding durbar in Hasina's concert hall, he quietly retires to Gulab's room by 8 p.m., long before the others wrap-up for the night.

One day, Qasem Khan took Hasina and Gulab to his own house, near Bowbazar. A double-storeyed structure with a garden enclosed by a high, concrete boundary. The large, high-ceilinged bedroom was attached to a wide veranda. One third of the veranda was surrounded by grilled iron bars, and that turned the bedroom into a near-fortress.

There was a reason for that. Inside his bedroom, a part of the wall had built-in almirahs that stored precious diamonds, rubies, emeralds and pearls. In terms of money they could total to a few crores of rupees.

The entire house was like a fort. At least six gun-wielding men were on guard. Then there were other servants and maids. But he had no wife.

Gulab Banu was overwhelmed but for some reason, Hasina returned with furrowed brows.

While bidding them good-bye, Qasem said, 'Bai Saheba, this house is yours too and I am at your service, a servant.'

'Shukriya, Khan Saheb,' Hasina smiled. 'Thank you.'

In the course of their conversation, Qasem Khan had learnt that Rabiya's departure had left Hasina inconvenienced. She had yet to find a replacement. Next morning Gulab informed her mother that Khan Saheb would send a woman to serve Hasina.

That very evening a woman around thirty years old, named Ruksana, came to Hasina and saluted her. She had been sent by Khan Saheb to serve her needs, she informed Hasina.

A few exchanges with her pleased Hasina. Ruksana had no one save an eleven-year-old son and an aged mother. Her husband had divorced her two years ago and now lived elsewhere.

'No more problem now?' Hasina queried.

'Jee, no!' Ruksana smiled.

She was engaged by Hasina. It turned out that she was a resourceful woman of happy mien. Intelligent too—she spoke after considerable thought. Apparently prior to this, she used to serve an English lady, and had to seek this employment because the lady had gone back to England.

A month has gone by. Qasem Khan comes and goes.

When this elderly but strong and handsome man is a bit late to arrive, Gulab Banu gets restless.

That was a Monday.

Qasem rose early from bed. The moment she sensed that the warmth next to her was missing, Gulab too came out of her sleep. She opened her eyes to see Khan Saheb was getting dressed to go out.

She was taken aback. 'What's this? You're already leaving, Saheb?'

Laughing aloud, Khan said, 'I have to rush today, my love. Very many people are expected in the office today. And then I have to leave for Murshidabad. I have some business there. I'll be back after a week to admire your moon-like face.'

Gulab Banu sat up in her bed. 'No.'

Qasem Khan smiled. 'Bibi, there's a lot of money to be earned. Once I'm back, I'm all yours.'

Gulab jumped out of her bed, ran to Qasem, hugged him and entreated, 'Go after a few days to make a pot of money, Saheb.'

Qasem silenced her with his lips.

He simply had to go, Qasem explained to Hasina Bai and took leave.

'Good thing,' Hasina said to her dispirited daughter. 'You can get some rest. Go to Naghma, chat with them, enjoy these few days.'

Gulab liked what her Ammi said. Her face brightened. In the afternoon she took Naghma and went to visit Zohra. They too had time on their hands. The three gossiped and giggled away to glory. They decided to spend the next three days at Zohra's place, shopping, chatting, drinking, snacking on ribald details of their nights.

Two days later. There was no mujra, and her daughter was away having fun with Zohra and Naghma. The house was quiet.

Ruksana came to look up Hasina. 'Do you need anything, Bibiji?'

'Yes,' Hasina was pleased. 'Get me a bottle of whisky from the cupboard, glasses, water, roasted grams and pakoras.'

'Right away, Bibiji.' In no time she had everything neatly organized. 'Any other command, Bibiji?'

'No, Ruksana. I'll call you if I need anything.'

Hasina poured herself a drink and took a generous sip. Today she's feeling rather lonely. If only there was a person she could love! Someone who would crush her into his chest, the way that—that Pratap Singh did!

He had been on her mind these past few days. In fact, since the day she noticed that scar on Qasem Khan's back.

She travelled back seventeen years to recall her own nath-utarna night. It was a spring day, in the month of Phalgun. The warm southern breeze was playing about her room. It was like the warm touch of a loving hand. Pratap, Pratap, Pratap.

She retraced how she had requested Uday to go to Bakhtiarpur in Bihar in search of Pratap Singh. He had gone there, spent a fortnight investigating, then returned to Calcutta and informed Hasina Bai that Pratap had disappeared but the villagers had found the dead body of his stepbrother in the jungles. His father had had a heart attack on hearing this. The British Police surmised that this was Pratap's doing—he had done away with his stepbrother Janardan in order to seize the entire property. No one could trace him after that; nor could Hasina get any news of him. Hai Pratap!

A small incident from that first night has been nagging her. When she was enjoying bliss through union with Pratap Singh, her ecstatic hold on him led to her fingers suddenly detecting uneven skin covering a deep scar. Precisely on the top right-hand corner of his back, near the shoulder…

After climaxing, when she was lying by his side spent and happy, she told him, 'My precious, I want to cuddle your beautiful back.'

'Really?' Pratap Singh had laughed. 'But don't stay riveted to my back!'

She had seen it up close then, the scar on his back. Caressing the spot she wanted to know, 'How did you wound yourself here, Saheb?'

'I fought with an enemy,' Pratap had jocularly explained. 'He stabbed me with a knife there.'

'Poor dear!' Hasina had kissed the scar. 'And then?'

'The enemy fled. I suffered for two months.'

'Has the enemy not been found by the police?'

'No. But he was found five-six months later, in the river, head severed from his body.'

'Who killed him?'

Pratap had laughed out loud. 'Must be an enemy of his.'

Hasina had guessed who that unnamed enemy was.

And after she got to know the history of the scar, the next time Pratap embraced her, she felt a strange high. Pratap, oh Pratap!

Ruksana entered the room in rapid steps. She came close to Hasina and reverentially said, 'Baisaheba, Qasem Khan Saheb is here.'

'How come?' Hasina stood up on faltering feet. 'Where have you seated him?'

'In Gulabji's room. He has brought lots of flowers, and gifts.'

'All right, I'll join him in a little while. Till then you tend to his needs.'

Ruksana left to do that.

Hasina stood on her feet, thinking. Then she came to a decision. Her eyes reflected her resolve. She emptied the drink in her glass. She put away the bottle she was drinking from, and brought out a more potent spirit. Then she rushed to the mirror and quickly applied surma under her eyes. A dash of costly attar on her earlobes and chest, and she was ready to leave the room.

Sitting in a chair, Qasem Khan was deep in thought. He turned around at the sound of footfall and found Hasina Bai standing before him. 'Salaam Walaikum, Khan Saheb!'

Respectfully Qasem stood up. 'Walaikum Salaam, Bai Saheba,' he returned her salutation.

'Take a seat,' Hasina responded. 'So you didn't go to Murshidabad?'

'No, Bai Saheba,' he spoke while returning to his chair. 'Just as I was to start off, I got the news that the person I was to meet in Murshidabad was in Barrackpore. So I went there and in two days finished what would otherwise have taken the rest of the week. Got back a little while ago.'

'Did you have a successful trip?' Hasina queried.

'Yes, by Khuda's meherbani, I surpassed expectations.'

'Bahut khoob! Excellent!' Hasina exulted. The next moment there was regret in her voice.

'But you'd said you would be gone for a week! So Gulab has gone to see her friends. She is at Zohra's place, Naghma is with her too.'

'Yes, that's what I heard,' Qasem smiled. 'Good for Gulab. Well then, I'll take leave. Maybe tomorrow…'

'What are you saying, Khan Saheb! How can you leave? I will immediately send for Banu.'

Qasem forcefully shook his head. 'No, Bai Saheba. It's already late. Poor thing, let her enjoy herself. I can return…'

'No, Khan Saheb, this is your house too. Stay the night here. We will take good care of you. I will get Gulab back first thing in the morning—'

As she spoke, Hasina came close to Qasem Khan. Close enough for him to be overpowered by the smell of her body, accentuated by the spicy attar, and the alcohol she had imbibed.

Qasem looked at Hasina's face, then humbly added, 'All right, Bai Saheba, as per your wish I will stay back and add to your bother.'

'Don't even think that! You are a son-in-law, dulha of this household. Just wait, I will organize every comfort for you in a jiffy.'

Hasina went out to instruct Ruksana to fetch the bottle of whisky from her room and everything else needed to make it enjoyable: glasses, ice, snacks. 'Speed it up,' she hurried her. She also sent Fatima to ask Uday Moinuddin if he would oblige by playing the sarangi for an hour. In her room, at a high pitch.

Then she returned to Qasem. By now Ruksana had brought everything she could have asked for.

Hasina sat in a chair close to Qasem Khan and assured him, 'No worries now. Sit back and relax with a drink, Khan Saheb.'

'Meherbani, Bai Saheba.'

Hasina poured a large drink in a silver glass and handed it to him. 'Here, Khan Saheb.'

'Bai Saheb, why don't you have a drink as well?'

Hasina cast a seeking glance at Khan, then protested, 'Oh no, we are not in that kind of equation.'

'Bai Saheba, when you drink alone, you feel sorry for yourself,'

Khan spoke modestly. 'That's why I requested you. Besides that, in your world of music and dance, the equations are different from those of ordinary householders. You are far more liberal.'

With that he reached out and touched Hasina's left arm with his right hand. 'Do give me company, Bai Saheba.'

Hasina smiled a very endearing smile. Qasem felt as if Gulab had smiled.

She said, 'There is logic in what you are saying, Saheb, so I will join you for this evening.'

At once Qasem poured another large portion in a glass and held it out for Hasina. 'Please accept, Bai Saheba.' Then he cast a reptilian look at her.

Hasina squarely met the creepy look in his eyes. She took the drink from his outstretched hand. As she did so, her fingers carelessly touched Qasem's and rested there for a few seconds. Then she raised the glass to her lip, without shifting her kinky gaze.

Qasem too raised his glass with no change in his insidious eyes and muttered, 'Victory to thee! May you win.'

'May you be captivated.'

Qasem emptied his glass at one go. Hasina also took a big gulp and said, 'So tell me Khan Saheb—'

'Tell you what?' Qasem asked, still not taking his eyes off her, and took another sip of his drink.

'You are into diamonds and rubies. Why not tell me about them?'

'Your wish is my command, Bai Saheba.'

Meanwhile Ruksana and Fatima replenished the snacks on the table in the room. Hasina gestured to them to leave. 'I will call you if we need anything else.'

'Jee Huzurain.' Ruksana cast a cagey look at Qasem Khan. As she left, she discreetly shut the door.

Thus started fascinating stories of Golconda diamonds, Burmese rubies, Nepalese garnets, Basra pearls. Yellow sapphire, white sapphire, blue sapphire, moonstone, turquoise, emeralds—which of these defines your destiny? Which one averts disasters? Which famous people have made which of the gems famous?

As the tales kept unfolding, the second drink was emptied.

Pouring himself a third drink, Qasem Khan studied Hasina, trying to gauge her condition.

Hasina too was not blinking. A mystifying smile played on her lips. And the dark of her eyes glistened with a resolve.

Qasem sipped on his drink. So did Hasina. Then, munching on a piece of kebab she said, 'Enough of gems and jewelleries. Now let's have some other stories, Khan.'

Qasem was tickled. Hasina had addressed him as 'Khan'. She had dropped the formal 'Saheb'. He said, 'Whatever pleases you, Bai—I'll narrate just that.' With that he placed the palm of his left hand on Hasina's. Both hands were feverish.

'When did you come to Calcutta?' Hasina was curious.

Qasem picked up her other hand in his and replied, 'A year and a half now.'

'And where were you before that?'

'In different corners of Punjab…'

'Why Punjab? You are from Bihar, aren't you?'

Qasem Khan was thrown off-guard at that. With knitted brows he demanded, 'Who told you that I'm a Bihari? Not at all. I'm Punjab da puttar, a pukka Punjabi. At one time I was in Rawalpindi, later in Lahore, and the last few years in Amritsar…'

Hasina lowered her voice, 'Where were you initiated into our world?' Hasina was quite tipsy but with gritted teeth she kept a hold on her senses.

Like an angler, Qasem Khan too was alternately surrendering himself to the alcohol inside him, and then holding back.

Gulab Banu's mother, he thought to himself, is so much like Gulab Banu but with so much more experience and maturity. Her personality and beauty have the flavour of a mature whisky.

'So…? When was your first time?'

'In Lucknow. Since then, whenever I had time or could make time I've been to Delhi. I used to come down from Punjab in search of entertainment.'

Hasina bent forward, placed her hand on his and purred, 'Why, Khan? Were you not well entertained at home?'

Qasem moved closer to Hasina, pressed her hand and said in a hushed tone, 'Bai, the pleasure your world offers is nirala, of its own kind. It's like a potent sharab…'

Hasina countered the pressure on her hand and asked in a gay voice, 'So which baiji do you still treasure in your memory?'

'Roopa Bai of Lucknow,' Qasem slurred.

'Did you take off her nath?'

'No, I had a three-month nikah arrangement with her.'

'And? Who else do you remember?' She was playing with his fingers, almost as if they were embracing each other. 'Go on Khan, open up.'

Qasem emptied his drink, put down the glass and turned to play with Hasina's fingers. 'And? And yes, I remember the tender and elegant Haseen—Zeenat!'

'You did her nath-utarna?'

'Oh yes! She was like a delicate cherub from the heavens, cute like Gulab Banu. Like—you. You are also angelic, gift from jannat… Give me some more wine, Hasina.'

Hasina poured another drink for him. Qasem poured some for her.

'Piyo Qasem—cheers!'

'Yes, cheers, Hasina.'

Just then Uday Moinuddin's sarangi floated in.

'Wah! Exquisite! The idiot plays well.' Qasem, unsteady on his feet, slurred in praise.

'What's he playing? Would you like to know?'

'Tell me, Zeenat.'

'This is Hasina Bai.'

'Right, right you are, Hasina. Go on, tell me, what is he playing?'

'It's a Kafi thumri. Have you heard the song?'

'Which song is it, Hasina?'

Hasina was not quite steady, but she got to her feet, and in a dancing posture she started singing softly in tune with Uday's sarangi, *Mere dard-e-jiger ki khabar nahin* (You know nothing about the pain in my heart... Oh heartless one, you do not care to know about my heartbreak).

Qasem swayed towards Hasina, put a hand around her and kept repeating in a drunken voice, 'Yes I do Hasina, I do Zeenat-e-Hasina...'

Hasina returned the embrace and said under her breath, 'And you are that same, my precious Pratap.'

Qasem did not reply. In his inebriated state of arousal he kissed Hasina on her lips, then he led her towards the bed and lay her on it.

Hasina forcefully sat up. She too was inebriated. 'What's the rush, dear? Let me first uncover you. It's a long way to dawn. Go slow jaan, my very breath—relish the moment.'

'Very well Hasina, let me be your toy. Go on, play as you wish.'

'Yes, take off your kurta.'

'Here, it's yours, sweetie. Take it,' he took it off.

'What bliss!' Hasina planted a kiss on his chest. 'Qasem, I want to kiss your back too!'

'Go on. That's yours too.' With a drunken laugh he turned his back to Hasina. She patted his back and quietly said, 'Your back is still beautiful. Do you remember that I had kissed this scar near your shoulder?' Promptly she kissed the spot.

Qasem was beyond control. 'Yes, Hasina yes, yes…'

'You took off my nath, remember?'

'I remember, Hasina! Hasina,' Qasem held her in his arms and again tried to lay her down in bed. But no sooner had he pulled her than Hasina cried out, 'Aah! Qasem—it's paining—my heart—Qasem let go of me… Oof! L-e-t g-o…'

'What's the matter, Hasina?' Qasem was startled, scared.

Hasina placed her hand on her breast and moaned, 'My heart is not in good shape. The hakim has cautioned me, the minute it aches, I must take my medicines. And I must lie down.'

'Don't worry, it will pass, Hasina. You rest your head on my chest.'

'No Qasem, you take rest. Oof! How painful!' Hasina ran to the door and shut it as she went out.

Qasem was dumb-founded. Suddenly he came to himself and through gritted teeth uttered an abuse.

Ruksana entered the room. 'Huzoor, if you need anything, please command me. Bai Saheb is feeling unwell. She just took some medicines and is lying in her bed.'

Qasem looked at Ruksana angrily. 'No, I won't need anything. You better go to your Bai Saheba.'

He lay down in the bed and right then Uday's sarangi stopped playing.

The next morning Qasem woke up pretty late. He was still lazing when Ruksana came in with tea.

'How's Hasina Bai feeling today?' he enquired.

'She has woken up but feeling tired.'

'Hunh…'

Qasem had the tea and quickly got dressed. When he was thinking of sending for Hasina, she herself walked in.

'Aadab, Khan Saheb.'

'Aadab. How are you feeling? Recovered?'

Hasina spoke in a mild voice, 'Not too well, Pratap.'

Qasem arched his brows. 'Who's Pratap?'

'You,' Hasina asserted.

'What's the drama about? My name is Qasem Khan!'

A smile played on Hasina's lips, 'And it's a truth that you are also Pratap Singh.'

'That is a Hindu name. I am a Muslim.'

The smile didn't leave Hasina. 'You killed your stepbrother and, to escape the law, you fled to Punjab and became a Muslim and made a fortune.'

Qasem raised his voice, 'Hasina Bai, you are insulting me. Listen to me Bai, you send for your daughter. I still have a right over her. I will be here tonight.'

'No Pratap, you will not come back, because Gulab Banu is your daughter. Once you have learnt this truth, you cannot sin again.'

'Sin?' Qasem roared. 'Can you prove that I am not Qasem Khan? Listen to me, Hasina. I am not Gulab Banu's father, I am the man who took her virginity.'

'Sixteen years ago you took my virginity. The stab-wound which Janardan Singh had inflicted on Pratap Singh's back is the same scar you carry on your shoulder. To unravel the truth, I went through the entire drinking charade last evening. No Pratap, I cannot allow you to sin with our daughter.'

'Sin!' Qasem Khan alias Pratap Singh pulled a face. 'Your entire life is made up of sins, baiji. The same man sleeping with the mother and the daughter is quite common amongst you. You know that as much as I do. Although, in this instance, your entire accusation is born out of your imagination. It is purely fictitious. So hear my final words: I will be back tonight and Gulab Banu should be here and waiting for me.'

Hasina replied equally firmly, 'You hear me, Qasem Khan. I had a suspicion that you are Pratap Singh. That is why I led you to bare yourself last night. Now when I am convinced that I am right in my belief, I will not let the sin repeat itself under my nose while I am alive. You too must submit to Khuda's laws.'

Qasem Khan was sceptical. 'A baiji is just a kasbi, another form of prostitute. You are ruled by Iblis, Satan, not by Khuda. I am giving you a final warning, Hasina Bai: I will be here in the evening, and if I don't find Gulab here I will abduct you.'

He spat out the words and swiftly disappeared. Hasina stood transfixed, listening to the receding sound of his carriage. When she made to leave the room, the fleeting shadow of Ruksana moved away from the door.

Hasina directly headed for Uday's quarters.

He was tending to the strings of his sarangi. He lifted his eyes, 'Hasina Bai?'

She slumped down next to him, 'Grave danger, Uday!'

V

True to his words, Qasem Khan showed up after sunset. With him were two gun-toting bodyguards and following in a separate car were eight men wielding lathis.

Qasem got off his carriage to find six constables with the red turban of the Imperial Police on duty—waiting with guns in their hands.

'Stop! Step no further!' the police chief ordered.

Qasem Khan stepped forward. 'I am the diamond merchant Qasem Khan. I am the son-in-law of this household. I must enter the building.'

The red-turban nodded in dissent. 'No, you are not to enter this building. By the order of the government.'

Tabla player Naseer Khan was watching through an open window. He saw Qasem Khan study the house for some minutes, then walk back to his carriage.

'Let's go back,' he commanded his coachman. The lathi-wielding security men followed in the other carriage.

However, at this point of the day Hasina Bai was not present in the building. Nor had Gulab Banu returned from her friend's place. They were both in hiding, in a safe house in Dumdum belonging to Kulsum Bai.

And the gun-wielding constables? They had been engaged by the same Harold Saheb and his English mem.

That very day Uday had accompanied Hasina to their house—and fortunately found him still holding the office of power. At once he sent an order for police protection and assured them that he would set in motion a process to uncover Qasem Khan's past.

At night, cooped up in a room in Kulsum Bai's resort, Gulab Banu confronted her mother. 'Ammi, tell me, what is the matter? Don't keep anything from me. I can sense that something has gone terribly wrong.'

'Yes dear, something is seriously wrong.'

'What is it, Ammi?'

Slowly, scanning every word, she spoke, 'Something terrifyingly unnatural, an accident, truly speaking…'

Gulab was tremulous, 'Go on Ammi, don't hesitate…'

'Full seventeen years ago a person had performed my nath-utarna. He was called Pratap Singh. He's your father. And seventeen years later that same person ended my daughter's virginity. Now he goes by the name of Qasem Khan.'

Gulab Banu turned into stone.

After a long spell of speechlessness she uttered in disbelief, 'No, Ammi!! No-o-o. NO.'

Hasina remained firm, 'Yes darling, yes. This is the truth. But you have not sinned baby, because let alone you, even I did not recognize him. For, in these intervening years he has put on weight. He has grown a full beard and moustache to proclaim his allegiance to Islam, and the exposed areas of his face are pockmarked. I came to identify him gradually, and carefully. Would you like to know how I am so sure?'

Hasina narrated, Gulab listened in silence. She stared vacantly into the air even after Hasina fell silent. Then she let out a howl. She plunged her head in her mother's lap and spat out, 'Chhee! Shame! Chhee chhee…'

Hasina hugged her tightly and held her close to her chest. Gulab's face was soaked in tears. 'Ammi,' she said hoarsely, 'I feel like destroying myself!'

Hasina silenced her with her hand. 'God forbid! You are my only sunshine in life, darling.'

A month went by. Hasina and Gulab Banu returned to their house.

Commissioner Harold sent a warning to Qasem Khan through a trusted constable that he should in no way be the cause for any bother to either Hasina Bai or her daughter Gulab Banu. He halved the number of gun-toting policemen guarding Hasina's house from four to two. He also summoned Uday and instructed him to relieve Ruksana from Hasina's employment as she was recommended by Qasem Khan.

Ruksana was paid a hefty baksheesh in addition to her salary, and a full set of new clothing. She left with tears in her eyes.

An uneasy sense of foreboding hung over the household. There was no singing, no dancing, no music played in the house.

Hasina Bai was toying with the idea of starting anew, with Gulab Banu's performance. She had to ensure that her daughter earned a good reputation and got a standing in the profession. But Gulab Banu was a withered blossom. She was unwilling to do any mujra yet. 'Let some more days pass, Ma,' she pleaded every time her mother proposed a concert.

Hasina felt sorry for her daughter. Every night, in the solitude of her bedroom, she poured a drink for herself and sat wondering how rapidly everything had gone for a toss. Her darling daughter, bursting with life and laughter, had turned into a shadow of herself. A pall of mourning seemed to have descended on the house where only the other day the corridors resounded with laughter and glee.

Barring Hasina Bai, Gulab Banu and Uday Moinuddin no one had an inkling of what exactly had transpired but everyone intuitively knew that some catastrophe had befallen them.

About ten days after Ruksana was fired, she re-appeared a little before sunset. She had found new employment in the Anglo neighbourhood, she was faring well. While at Hasina's, she used to share the room with Fatima at night. In the flurry of departure she had forgotten a box of her belongings in that room. She had come to pick up that box.

'Sure, take it with you,' Hasina was civil to her. 'How could you forget a whole box of belongings? Collect it from that room.' She summoned Fatima and instructed her to make it convenient for Ruksana to collect her stuff.

Fatima had developed an easy friendship with Ruksana. She seated her in the kitchen and offered her tea and biscuits. Later Ruksana went to her room, gathered the tin box forgotten atop an almirah, returned to the kitchen, chatted for a while longer and took her leave.

Dinner was over early that night. The perfectly circumscribed silver moon was casting a gossamer mesh of mystery in the air. So, after an interval of several weeks, Uday Moinuddin's sarangi started playing that unforgettable thumri, *Piya more Pardeswa...* But Hasina Bai felt stifled by the strain of that song. She was restless. Nothing, simply nothing was worth loving anymore. Uday was excelling in his usual skilled playing, still... Hasina was not entranced.

All of a sudden, the harmony of the sarangi was harshly ruptured by Gulab Banu's groans.

Her stomach was burning. She was doubling under the pain of a terrible ache. Neither she nor anyone else had a clue what had brought it on. As her screams reached his ears, Uday stopped playing his sarangi and joined Hasina and all the others who had crowded outside Gulab's door.

Hakim Ajmal Khan came in no time. He personally administered some medicines, but to no effect. Gulab Banu kept tossing and turning on her bed, she bolted upright clutching at her tummy, she kicked the air and hit out at the vacant space that seemed to be suffocating her. Hasina started howling. Clutching the hakim's feet she kept screaming, 'Save her, Hakim Sa'ab save my daughter!' Uday scampered to the English neighbourhood of Chowringhee and returned with the reputed English doctor Jacob. By then Gulab Banu had wilted. She was in a semi-conscious state, her eyes drooping. Naseer Khan had started reciting the Quran. It was the last lap of the night.

Jacob examined Gulab with great care. 'Sorry,' he shook his head, 'it is too late…' Still he gave her an injection and waited for it to yield some result. In a short while, foiling every attempt to revive her, Gulab fell silent.

Jacob felt her pulse. Hakim Sa'ab too felt her pulse. They shook their heads. 'Yaa Khuda!' was all that was heard. Jacob stood up and left the room in stony silence. Before the light of dawn could enter her room, Gulab Banu's lifebreath exited the world. The sixteen-year-old would sing or dance no more.

Hasina fell to the floor, unconscious.

The next day.

Word spread like wildfire through the world of baijis. Every tawaif worth her name visited Hasina. In the falling light of the day the bewitching beauty of Gulab Banu was laid to rest six feet under the soil.

All was over. Dust unto dust…

VI

Commissioner Harold informed Uday, 'Moinuddin, Ruksana is untraceable at this moment, but I shall not rest until she is arrested.'

'And Qasem Khan?' Uday asked. 'Ruksana was merely putty in his hand…'

'I know,' Harold seemed worried. 'He is very clever, and unfortunately he has quite a formidable reputation in the market. Above all he has pots of money. So we have to be discreet in carrying out our investigation. That is why it is crucial to apprehend Ruksana.'

Uday returned home and reported it all to Hasina. She didn't utter a single syllable.

Days passed by. Nights came and went.

The agents and pimps stopped frequenting the premises. 'Jinxed'. The market put this sobriquet before Hasina's name. Now every seth and babu would think twice before visiting her.

But Uday and the other musicians didn't let any such gossip reach Hasina. On her part, Hasina too didn't care to know anything. Once in a while Kulsum Bai, Ruksana and Nadira Bai would come and sit with her in silence, then leave after some hours. Hasina had no inclination to dress up. Every now and then she would roam around the house and through the rooms. Once in a while she would go to Gulab's bedroom, open her almira, touch her salwar kameezes, feel her ghaghras, hold her ankle bells to her chest, rest them on her cheek… She would lie down on her daughter's bed, sit upright and then walk out of the room, go downstairs to Uday's room and sit in a chair, or would go sit with Naseer Khan's wife Noor. The moment Noor would try to caress and console her, she would hastily depart. She would roam about like a phantom and now and then wail, 'Oh my darling, Gulab… Oh my cherry, Gulbanu…' Invariably this would remind her of Gulab's sire and she would spit hatred—'Iblis! Diabolic son of Lucifer! Devil incarnate…'

Every single inmate of the house could hear her lament and tears welled up in every single eye. They would tremble in fear for Hasina.

Days went by.

But how long could Jhanu Mullick and Sagiruddin and Naseer Khan remain idle? The rosiest of the blossoms in the market had been murdered by Qasem Khan—demon, beast, worse than an animal, Satan, no less. Hasina has no heart to sing and dance anymore. Nor was there any craze for her in the market. So what could the players do? True, Hasina was still paying their salaries but for how long would she continue? Day and night, like an apparition, she would flit about from room to empty room, all by herself.

That morning she decided to drop by Uday's. He was reading the Geet Govind. Startled to see her walk in, he rose to his feet and welcomed her, 'Good to see you, Bai Saheba.'

Hasina did not reply. She sat down in a chair and kept staring at the wall facing her.

Uday put aside the book in his hand and fixed his gaze on Hasina. She did not even notice this. After a while had passed, Uday mumbled, 'Bai, calm down. Get a hold of yourself. Surrender to the will of Khuda.'

Hasina showed no sign of hearing him. Then she mumbled, 'I have surrendered myself in your hands, Khuda! What else can I do except lower my head in your court!'

She fell silent. Moments lapsed. Then she sprang to her feet and addressed the Almighty again, 'But Ae Khuda, why should my daughter's killer go unpunished? That heinous sinner—why let him off? Why won't you destroy him, Allah?'

She darted out of the room even before her cry had melted into the air.

Uday sat motionless in silence. Stony silence.

Until Jhanu Mullick, Sagiruddin and Naseer Khan entered in a group. Uday was on his feet again, 'Come. Come, take a seat.'

Naseer Khan took the lead. 'Uday, spare yourself the trouble to be hospitable. We need to discuss something with you. In fact, we need your advice.'

'What about, Dada? Tell me.'

Now Jhanu Mullick spoke on behalf of the group. 'The market is buzzing with rumours to the effect that it is the end for this house. That no one comes here now nor will anyone book Bai for any concert. In these last two months Bai has not done a single mujra but has paid us on time. But what good is the salary if we can't play? We will have no market, no one will invite us to play if we are not heard. We have to think about our reputation, our future, and of our families. So tell us, what should we do?'

Uday was lost in thought for a short while. Then he said, 'Give me a couple of days, sirs. Hold your peace for three days…'

No one spoke into the uneasy silence. It was Uday who spoke again, 'This afternoon I will visit the dargah of the Pir at Mirpur, Mullick Dada.'

Naseer Khan was pleased to hear this. 'That's good. Yes, go and pay your respect to the Pir…'

'Yes, I wish to pray at the dargah. These next few days be alert. Do tell the lathiyals and darwans also to stay on guard. Bai Saheb is still not out of danger. The enemy is of the worst kind. But be kind enough not to tell her that I am leaving for Mirpur.'

'Well then,' Jhanu Mullick spoke for the rest, 'we will watch out and also guard Bai Saheb. You pray for the welfare of all of us and come back soon, Uday.'

Four days went by.

Hasina never sleeps, it would seem. Less than forty winks, and she is up with a start. Isn't that Gulab calling out to her, 'Ammi—O Maa—'

The fifth evening she heard herself being addressed by a low voice, 'Bai Saheba!'

With a start she asked, 'Who is it?'

Uday Moinuddin showed up at the door. Dishevelled, unshaven, dark lines under his eyes, a thaili on his shoulder bulging with considerable weight.

Hasina briskly walked up to the door, 'Where were you these past four days, Uday? Where had you disappeared?'

'I'd gone to Mirpur,' Uday replied in the same low voice, 'to the dargah of the Pir…'

'That's good, but why didn't you tell me that?'

'That was a lapse, Bai.'

'Why are you standing at the door? Come and sit inside.'

'No, Bai Saheba,' Uday shook his head, 'I don't have the time. I must leave forthwith.'

Hasina fell from the sky. 'Where will you go now? And why? What's the matter with you?'

'That's what I'm here to tell you, Hasina Bai. I want you to know that you should not fear for any harm from that enemy of yours. The Almighty who judges every wrong has meted out his punishment. That beast is no more.'

'What did you just say?' Hasina stepped forward. 'My enemy…?'

'Qasem Khan alias Pratap Singh now dwells beyond the clouds…'

'How do you know that?' Hasina's voice trembled, perhaps out of fear. But Uday's voice was strangely calm. 'Thus far I alone know this. Slowly, gradually, the entire city will get to hear about his death.'

Hasina stood right next to Uday. 'You…him…did you…?' Her voice trailed off.

'Yes, Bai,' Uday whispered, 'I was the sceptre in the hands of the Almighty.'

Wide-eyed Hasina had forgotten to blink.

'I must get going, Bai,' Uday sought to bid goodbye. 'Else, we will all be in deep trouble. This very night I will leave Calcutta.'

'How can you?' Hasina was troubled at the thought. 'Where will you go?'

'I haven't given that a thought. I have had no time to think.'

Suddenly Hasina grabbed his hand and pulled Uday into her room. Then, she shut the door before asking. 'Has anyone seen you?'

'I have no idea but the English policemen are quite alert, relentless.'

'How will you live? What will you do for a living?'

'I will make my home in a village and take to farming. Never again will I play the sarangi—its strain will give me away. Now bid me goodbye, Bai. You have nothing to fear or worry about anymore. Still, be careful…' Uday made for the door.

'Wait, Uday!'

He turned around, 'Yes, Bai?'

'Where are you headed now?'

'To the residence of Haripada Sil. He repairs my sarangi and has deep affection for me. I will spend the day in his quarters and depart after nightfall.'

'Will you see me before leaving town?'

'It is perilous for me to be seen in this building, Bai Saheba.'

'So where can I see you?' Hasina firmly asked. 'Somewhere close by?'

Uday thought for a moment, then replied, 'Outside Thanthaniya Kalibari.'

'Well thought. Good. That is where I will see you.'

'But why do you want to see me?'

'Because Hamidan Khala had left her jewellery in my safekeeping. Besides, I wish to give you some money for the new chapter of your life. You have earned it. It will not be right to send these through Naseer Chacha or anyone else. That will compromise your safety.'

'Quite right. But you will come out all alone at night?'

'No, I won't,' Hasina reassured him. 'Fatima will be with me. I will leave her somewhere close by and come to you.'

'Okay then, do just that.'

Hasina needed one clarification. 'What should I do with your belongings?'

Uday handed over the keys to his rooms. 'Do whatever you consider right. I'm giving you that responsibility. My final word is that I will be outside the temple at 11 p.m.' He paused, then said, 'May I leave, Bai Saheba?'

'Go ahead,' Hasina softly responded. Uday parted the door carefully, peeped outside to make sure the corridor was clear, and left.

Immediately Hasina got busy. So much to do! So much to take care of…

An hour after Uday had departed, when Hasina opened her trunk and sat picking out the jewellery Hamidan Khala had entrusted her with, she heard Naseer Khan outside her door, 'Hasina, my child!'

She shut the trunk and opened the door to find fear writ on their faces as they walked into her room. A worried Hasina asked, 'What's the matter, Chacha?'

'The city is agog with stories, Bai!' Jhanu Mullick burst out, 'Someone has murdered Qasem Khan!'

'Haey!' Hasina pretended to be shocked. 'What catastrophe is this?'

'Yes, child,' Naseer Khan chimed in, 'Qasem Khan was part of our lives. Just the other day our baby was killed…'

Silence ruled the room. Jhanu Mulllick ruptured it. 'Uday isn't back from the Pir's dargah yet. That, too, is a cause for concern.'

'Why worry?' Hasina tried to console her uncle. 'Neither of us has poisoned our baby or Qasem Khan. Whatever is Allah's will, will come to pass, Chacha. Do keep praying that the Munificent One protects us all.'

Though still anxious, Naseer Khan agreed with Hasina. 'You're right, child. God's will rules the world.'

Slowly they walked down the stairs to their quarters. Hasina shut the door to her room.

Thanthania Kalibari. At 11 p.m.

The temple had still not been deserted by devotees. A gaslight was shining at the corner of the street. A little distance away, standing in the shadows of a veranda, Uday was keeping a sharp eye on the road. He took out an English watch from his shirt-pocket. Yes, it was 11 p.m.

The temple bell was sounding again and again, almost every time a voice raised its pitch to say, 'Jai Maa!'

All of a sudden a burqa-clad woman materialized out of nowhere and addressed him, 'Uday Moinuddin!'

Immediately she lifted her veil to show her face. Hasina Bai stood before him with a large bag on her shoulder.

'Have you decided where to go from here?' she wanted to know.

'Yes, I have,' Uday confided in her. 'I will walk up to Srirampur, then take a train to Odissa, then proceed to Hyderabad. That is the Nizam's territory. I might be somewhat safe there.'

'That is a good roadmap.'

'Where have you left Fatima waiting for you?'

'I haven't brought her along. I am here by myself.'

'Why?'

'Because I don't need her anymore. I cleared everybody's dues today. Naseer Chacha's, Jhanu Kaka's, Sagiruddin Chacha's… every single person's. I paid the landlord two months' rent in advance and vacated the house. Two months down, if the Chachas can afford the rent, they will continue to stay on there…'

'But why, Hasina Bai?' Uday could not quite grasp what she was saying. 'Why will you vacate the house?'

'Because I am no longer a "Bai", Uday,' Hasina softly replied. 'From now on I am merely Hasina. The sin accumulated over four generations of being baijis cost me the life of my Gulab. It has ended with her death. Today I have liberated myself from that life of sin.'

'What are you saying, Hasina? What does it imply?'

Hasina smiled. 'Only today did I realize for how long you have been showering your love on me. You have made so many sacrifices for this love. You have put up with all my indifference and tolerated neglect. You have always served every need of mine.

And you have given me the ultimate offering by settling the score with the sinner who offended the dignity of both me and my daughter. With this act you have turned me into your slave for life. My baby's death has opened my eyes to our life, Uday!'

'Hasina!' Uday was overwhelmed.

Hasina's voice choked with emotion as she said, 'Don't turn me away, Uday!'

Uday was startled by the use of the intimate 'tui', which she used to address him in her childhood. But he kept his calm. 'Hasina, many in this city have by now learnt that Qasem Khan has been murdered. If the police trace me, your life will also be in danger.'

'I will peacefully face that danger, Uday! Don't punish me by turning me away.'

Uday stepped forward and took her hand in his. 'Finally Govind has filled the emptiness in my heart! Well then, let's start out on a new life in the name of God. May Khuda protect us on this journey!'

With her eyes streaming tears, Hasina firmly held on to Uday's grip on her hand. 'Let's go, Uday. Now onwards I will be the sarangi you have left behind.'

'Let's set out,' Uday said, his voice tinged with the warmth in his heart.

The temple bell was still resonating the prayers of the Devi's devotees when Uday and Hasina took to the road ahead, hand in hand.

When they reached a somewhat sparsely populated space, they could see the waning moon of the dark fortnight. Perhaps to light up their journey, the moon started to walk with them.

In their heart, Uday and Hasina could hear his ancestor bless them: 'Well done! After all the drama in your lives you have admitted your love for each other. You are still dogged by danger. Still, keep faith in hope, and keep loving. Keep spreading love…'

Translated from the Bengali by Ratnottama Sengupta

It Happened One Night

Tagar takes out her make-up kit. Just an hour ago heavy rains had lashed the lane. The sky is still overcast and the easterly wind is biting cold. But it's already five in the evening. Time seems to have flown past.

Unlike other days, Tagar has overslept. Panna did try to wake her up several times, but Tagar didn't get up. Yes, time is flying past.

Tagar places the kettle on the ramshackle stove in one corner of her room and starts to deck herself up. For the last seven years she has followed the same routine: she drapes herself in a blue zari-bordered sari, puts on some imitation jewellery and sticks a pale bindi on her forehead. She accentuates her eyes with a thin line of kohl, decorates her feet with a thick band of red alta, dusts herself with an inexpensive talcum powder, and signs off with a dab of 'Dilbahar'.

Her make-up done, Tagar stands in front of a large mirror hanging on the wall. Staying up late every night has taken its toll: she has dark circles under her eyes. Who knows what is etched on her forehead in an invisible script. If only she could read it! Her body isn't what it used to be. Her hour-glass waist has prospered, her breasts have become lax. But she's still attractive and can pull on for some more years. Yes, years.

The kettle has come to a boil. 'Is there a cup for me too?' Maanada is standing in front of Tagar. Middle-aged, plump, dark-complexioned, pockmarked, Maanada has seen a time when she was in great demand…but now!

'Take a seat, Didi!' Tagar says, handing her a cup of tea. As Maanada takes a sip, Tagar asks her, 'Have you seen Shashi?'

Maanada makes a face. 'Does that son of a bitch have any sense? He has been absconding since last night,' she blurts out. This seems to worry Tagar. 'Who knows where the rascal has gone?'

'Couldn't have gone very far,' Maanada smiles. 'Do you know how much he loves you?'

Tagar laughs out loud. This 'love' is an old story. Sudhir also 'loved' Vimla. That Vimla is today's Tagar. But where did that roguishly good-looking youth disappear?

Maanada has finished her tea. 'So long, Di!' she gets up to go. 'I too must get dressed.'

Maanada is back in her room. Life is not what it used to be. No one is drawn to her anymore. Now she lives like a slave. A slave to those she once competed with, in youth and beauty. Still she dresses up and stands at the door, trying to seduce the passers-by with suggestive glances and vulgar jokes. This routine has become a part of her being.

Maanada has left but Tagar is still sitting on her bed. Shashi loves her! But now she could not bring herself to laugh at the thought. Her eyes are glazed. Her thickly powdered forehead is creased with lines. From the corner of her eye, a teardrop wants to declare her misery. That old story: love!

The bright day has withered into an overcast, windswept evening. The hazy light blends well with the darkness of nightfall, creating pictures, reviving old memories.

She can hear Sudhir's voice: 'Vimla, I love you.'

Vimla is shy, tongue-tied. She cannot utter a single word.

The setting sun has sprinkled red on the clouds—they look dyed in the blood of a dead sun.

'Vimla, you are mine,' Sudhir again says.

'And you are mine,' Vimla purrs.

There's joy in the street. The damp easterly winds have carried the pleasant aroma of cooked meat from Kanhai's shop at the end of the narrow, winding lane.

Sudhir clasps Vimla in a tight embrace. 'Let's run away Vimla,' he says.

'Come, let's go,' she responds.

But at this point the dream shatters. The honeybee disappears, leaving Vimla heavy with his child.

Amidst the roving eyes feasting on her beauty, she could hear the crying of a newborn. And then…

'Who are you thinking of?'

Vimla is startled. Boonchi is standing in front of her.

It is well past dusk. The yellow light from the lamppost has thickened the night. The lane is bubbling with laughter and noise.

'Oh Black Rose! Whose thoughts are you lost in?'

Laughing raucously, Tagar replies, 'Oh come on, don't start ribbing me!'

'Do tell us, oh lady worthy of Indra, whose thoughts have taken you away from us?'

Boonchi had once essayed the role of a Sakhi, the handmaiden of the heroine in a jatra. That was her first and last attempt at acting. Her stage fright ensured that she could not utter a single word. One look at the audience, and her mouth went dry. But, all the dialogues she could not deliver that evening, she now recites in front of Panna, Tagar and Maanada—with dramatic exaggeration.

Tagar laughs heartily. 'Boonchi, you're very good.'

'Aren't you thinking of the man who stole your heart?' Boonchi persists.

Stole her heart? That mistake did happen once. But that's an old story. Now where's the need for a Purush Shrestha—a man for all seasons—in her life? Each day brings in new men: old, young, middle-aged, healthy, sick… They swarm in from every direction and hover around her—even now.

No, Tagar does not lose her heart to anybody. But Vimla sure did, once. However, that unfortunate Vimla is no more.

'Boonchi…'

'Yes, my lord? What does your heart desire?'

'Stop this gibberish.'

'Why, master of my life?'

'Just peep out of the window. They've all gone out.'

'Really!' Boonchi is startled. 'Come, let's go.'

They come out and stand on either side of the door. The streetlight lends a glitter to their clothes and jewellery. At the same time it bestows them with a celestial aura.

Nightfall presses the 'Start' switch of their lives. All of them, the five who live in the same bordello, come out and stand beneath the lights. Maanada stands among them. She can't but do this.

'Your youth is blooming every day, Tagar!' Panna laughs.

Tagar is silent for a while, and then joins in the laughter.

Suddenly her eyes fall on Radha leaning against the door. 'Radha! Why are you here?' Radha looks in her direction. 'Aren't you supposed to be on medicines and rest?'

'Yes. But I need money for that. Today my bariwali gave me a final warning. She'll throw me out on the street if I don't pay the rent.'

What can Tagar say to that?

Standing there like a corpse holding on to a pillar with rickety arms, Radha stares at the men walking the streets with her large, loveless eyes. Months of illness has made her body skeletal. Her dark complexion has lost its sheen. Her cheeks have lost their lustre. Her scalp has lost its crowning glory. Radha has been so ill that she breathes with extreme effort. In fact she has just days left to breathe. Dr Paresh has already sounded her third bell. But besides that final hour, she's waiting for somebody who'll give her some money. Tonight, she needs it.

'Radha, you go in and sleep,' Kanak says. 'Rest for a few more days before you step out.'

But Radha does not budge. She stands there—frozen, speechless.

'Bibijaan! This ghulam salutes you!'

A dark fat man in a mulmul kurta and Multani shoes has walked up to them. Panna giggles and steps forward. *'Mar, marduey*! *Yeh nakhra*… Come with me.' The man laughs lustily. Panna pushes him inside the room.

Slowly, the crowd surges in the lane which is bustling with energy, perfumes, powder and body odours. Varied faces, different attires, distinctive languages… Add to this the chuhalbaazi, cigarette smoke and paan ki peek.

'Oye, this woman is a patakha.'

'Who?'

'That one there—the girl with her hands on her waist. Aha! Look at her firm body. What an inviting stance!'—one man is telling another.

A young man casting furtive glances around him settles his gaze on Tagar. He walks up to her, stops in front of her and says, 'Here! Please listen to me.'

'Did you say something to me?' Tagar turns to face him with a smile.

'Who do you think he is talking to?' Boonchi is peeved.

The boy wipes off the perspiration on his forehead. It's a first time for him in this lane.

'So, what were you saying?' Tagar asks innocently.

'Let's go in.'

'Wah! First let's talk money.'

'That will come later.'

The women break into a lusty laugh. But a depressed Radha doesn't join in.

Tagar goes into the room and asks the young man to take a seat. He squats awkwardly, takes out a cigarette from his pocket and lights it, taking quick puffs.

'Care for a paan?' Tagar tries to break the ice.

'No, I don't chew paan.'

The boy is staring intently at Tagar. His nostrils flared. Still, you couldn't ignore his attractive looks. A newcomer on this path, Tagar smiles to herself.

'When did you enter this profession?' he asks her.

'What's the use of asking such questions? Do you wish to become another Devdas?'

The young man is embarrassed. 'No, I was just...'

'So, shall I switch off the light?'

'Okay,' he calls out from the bed and flicks his cigarette towards the veranda. 'You can switch it off now.'

'But first give me two rupees,' Tagar insists.

The rustling of two notes slices the silence in the room, then the light goes out. The darkness is a turn on, setting their blood on fire. His embrace nearly suffocates Tagar and seems to crush her body.

The cigarette lying in the veranda has gone out. The young man hangs his head, perhaps out of remorse. Running his fingers through his hair, he stands up.

'Can I have a cigarette?' Tagar pleads.

The youth buries his face in his hands. Then, in stony silence, he gives her a cigarette.

Tagar smiles at him. 'Why not stay a while longer?'

'No.' He sounds dejected.

'Don't you want to listen to my story?'

He vigorously shakes his head to say, 'NO.'

'Well then, come tomorrow...?'

He turns red with embarrassment. He stands still for a while, then strides towards the staircase.

Tagar laughs out loud. She knows he will return. Right now he's depressed; but when the blood coursing through his dull veins is in heat again, he will be back.

The smell of cooked meat wafts in from Kanhai's shop. Panna is laughing in the next room. The music coming in from Sukeshi's house across the street is melodious. The metropolis heaves a sigh in the arm of slumber.

Tagar looks into the mirror. She touches up her bun, straightens her sari and goes down the stairs.

Shashi returns home.

He takes four long strides up the stairs, and smiles at Tagar. 'I was looking for you,' he says.

'Why? What did you want from me?' Tagar angrily retorts. 'Something to eat?'

'No! Just two paise—' Shashi follows Tagar back to her room.

The light in the room shows Shashi wearing a kurta stitched out of an old sari. His dry hair is scattered all over his face. The tall and dark Shashi looks a little weak. His cheeks have caved in, giving his face a longish look. His cow-like eyes convey innocence, obedience and dismay—all at the same time.

While handing him the money Tagar takes a closer look at him. Her heart throbs in excruciating pain. How unfortunate Shashi is! When and in which dark lane was he born, from the womb of a prostitute? Even he doesn't know that. His unfettered, anchorless life in the midst of the brothel is an exercise to forget the event of his birth. When and where does he go? He is not aware, nor does he care about what he eats or drinks.

'Did you get a bite or not?'

'Haan,' Shashi nods his head, 'of course I've eaten.'

'What? Where?' A moment's pause. Again it's Tagar's voice, 'Shashi…'

'What?'

'Why are you rotting here? Why don't you work somewhere else?'

Suddenly Shashi's tired eyes brighten up. 'It's because of the blood ties,' he replies.

'Shashi, don't trash my words!'

'Never!' Shashi looks serious. 'I can never forget your affection.'

'Why so?'

Shashi has no answer to this. He thinks of something but does not speak his mind. Instead he says, 'Today at Ganesh's house I met an extraordinary person. He was not aged but was so knowledgeable! Something he said has left a deep impression on me.'

'What did he say?'

'I'll tell you. But before that, will you tell me something?'

'What?'

'Do you find this life acceptable?'

Tagar is taken aback by his question. Deep in thought, she slowly shakes her head and says, 'No. But what other means of livelihood do I have?'

Shashi has a dreamy look in his eyes as he says, 'That man said, there will soon come a day when none of you will lead this despicable way of life. The present social structure will crumble and a new society will emerge.'

Shashi's voice is trembling with emotion. He somehow finishes what he has to say, then stares out of the window.

Tagar does not get the full import of what he is saying but she likes what she hears. Society and man: It makes sense. For a moment her past comes alive. The emotional memories hide a touching story that shatters her from time to time.

With a high-pitched laughter she says, 'Well, then, let's go down.'

'Tagar!' Suddenly Shashi sounds excited.

'What?'

'Let's go, but not down. Let's leave behind this dog's life and run away from this dismal lane. Will you come?'

Tagar smiles indulgently. 'Black-faced, why do you take so much pity on me? Why not say this to Boonchi, Maanada or Panna?'

'Because I love *you*!'

'What?' Tagar recalls what Maanada said to her. Memories from her past start playing havoc with her emotions. Her face crinkles in agony. 'Love! Scoot,' she spits out. 'He wants to love a prostitute! How much money do you have in your pocket?'

Shashi's large eyes look like they will fall off their sockets. 'So what if I don't have money? The moneyed people come for an hour and leave. Our bond isn't like theirs. I am the son of a prostitute—if I don't love a prostitute, who can I love?'

'This is what happens if you pet a street dog,' Tagar says in a weary tone. 'Now that his stomach is full, Babusaheb is all set to talk love. Tell me, how many customers have you brought in today? Go away. Just get lost...'

Colour drains out of Shashi's face. He looks like a listless animal. Gritting his teeth he says, 'Yes, yes, I've asked an old man to wait outside. He's waiting there, for you...'

Tagar thinks for a moment. 'Go bring him in,' she says.

'I'll do that,' Shashi says, taking long strides towards the staircase. The lamp casts a slanting shadow on the stairs. In its pale light Tagar can see Shashi's eyes have filled up with tears. He looks back at her, as if to say something. What a strange creature this Shashi is, Tagar thinks to herself. 'Crazy!' she mutters aloud.

Tagar sits on the bed. A moist easterly wind is blowing into the room. The cloud-clapped sky is bereft of a single star. Shashi's love... Sudhir... Vimla... Tagar picks up the thread of memories from where it had snapped earlier that evening.

A city. A child was crying. Vimla's intoxication wore off. She realized she could not back off from where she had reached. Honeybees she had attracted were gathering around her. Their vulgar gestures conveyed dirty thoughts and coarse temptations. Lust. The heavy burden of sin would not leave her. Vimla was worried. What should she do? Where should she go?

One day she decided that all will be fine if the baby was dead. In a moment of madness she acted on that thought. Then she went to a forest faraway and buried the infant. But only after that she realized she had made permanent what she had wanted to forget.

Once seduced by love, a power beyond anyone's control, she decided to use that same power as her capital. She started a new life in this lane where use and abuse by a series of men turned Vimla into Tagar.

Nothing new in that story, Tagar thinks to herself as some footsteps approach her.

An old man, probably in his sixties, enters the room. His frail body is bent with the age that has turned grey half the hair on his head. He's wearing a pleated dhoti and kurta. A silk chaadar is adding to his composure though his narrow eyes express doubt.

'Come in,' Tagar says.

Shashi comes onto the veranda and peeps into the room.

'What are you saying?' the old man laughs. 'I'm already here.'

'Please take a seat.'

'Are you Tagar?'

'Yes—'

'So Shashi didn't lie to me. You're not bad looking!'

'Will you have a paan?'

'Sure! I've had paan so many times, why not from your hand? But don't do any tantra mantra please!'

'You are scared of black magic? Do I look like a tiger?'

'Tiger? You are a bigger cat than a tiger—you are bagh ki mausi,' he laughs heartily at his own joke.

Suddenly his eyes fall on the portrait of Kali hanging on a wall. His laughter evaporates. He averts his eyes and barks, 'At least switch off the light!'

'Why?' Tagar is rather surprised. 'Why this sudden hurry? Let's chat for a while.'

'I'm telling you—just switch off the light.'

The room plunges into darkness. 'Why this portrait of Maa Kali in this room?' his voice is harsh.

'Aren't we all children of the Mother?'

'No, that's not it. I'm scared to do anything in front of Her.'

'Well, then, go away.'

The man stretches out his arm and pulls Tagar's lax body towards him. 'Crazy girl, do people come here to go away?'

Tagar smiles as she says, 'Do you think Maa won't see what's happening if the portrait is gone?'

'Na—ah…but…'

'So you commit sins in this delusion and also delude yourself?'

'Stop talking big things,' he says tightly grasping her.

Shashi stands on the staircase. What is he thinking, this son of a prostitute?

The light comes back to life. The old man is wearing a pathetic smile. 'When the heat is off, I suffer from a sense of guilt. Why do I come here? I wonder!'

'Why do you say this?'

'What can I say to that? I can't control my own mind. I have daughters, daughters-in-law and grandchildren at home. But I can't help coming here. What am I to do?'

'You must be seeking romance,' Tagar smiles to him.

'But romance here is feigned—mere acting!'

The old man walks out of her room.

Romance—mere acting! Was Vimla's romance also mere acting? Tagar pondered over the thought for some time.

Radha is still standing as before. Not a single person has looked at her so far.

In another corner Maanada is also standing as before. She looks at Tagar and chips in, 'You are getting prosperous!'

'Why do you say that?'

'One man goes out, another comes in…'

Tagar smiles as she responds, 'Boonchi, Panna and Kanak are all in their rooms.'

Maanada looks at the street with longing in her eyes. Will someone be enamoured of her? There was a time when a crowd would be milling around her. There was this paunchy Marwari who fell at her feet pleading, 'Come away with me, please—' But she had not gone. And today? Maanada lifts her hand to feel her pockmarked face.

Tagar looks at Radha and feels a surge of affection. 'Radha—' she softly calls out.

A crestfallen Radha looks at her.

'If you need money, take it from me but give yourself some rest.'

Radha cannot bring herself to reply, she simply looks away.

As the hours progress the black veins of night pulsate with a dark soul. The lane throbs with people. Different faces, many languages, laughter, gestures, signs, alcohol, paan, and invisible germs laughing at the madness of men. The air is laden with the smell from Kanhai's shop. The night thickens.

Shashi comes back to her. 'I have brought another man,' he tells her.

An unsteady man walks behind Shashi. His hair is scattered

over his face. His dry cheeks have aged before their time. His drunken, meandering eyes are dancing hither and tither.

'Bring him in,' Tagar moves towards her room.

The stranger follows her. 'Why are you in such a rush?' he croaks. 'Let me at least take a good look at you.'

Tagar halts abruptly. Turning to the stranger she taunts him, 'Look na! How much do you want to look?'

'Wow, you look great—' the unstable stranger laughs out.

Tagar stares hard at him. Suddenly the blood in her veins starts to boil. Her inner being burns with a fire of revenge. She holds him by his neck and screams out, 'Shashi!'

Shashi's long shadow falls on the stairs.

'Take this bastard away from here.'

'Why?'

'Because I am telling you.'

The intoxication has drained out of the stranger. He leans against the wall and says, panting, 'You look somewhat familiar. What is your name?'

'Now there's no need to get familiar. I don't want to set eyes on you again, in this lane or anywhere else,' Tagar breaks into a hysterical laughter.

'But who are you?'

'Who else but the prostitute Tagar?'

'No no, tell me your actual name…'

'Shashi—' Tagar roars, 'didn't you hear what I said? Throw this dog out on the street!'

Shashi pushes the stranger out of the room.

Tagar sits down on the stairway.

Radha takes two men from Kabul to her room upstairs. Tonight she desperately needs the money.

Suddenly Tagar is back on her feet and scans the lane from one end to another. The stranger has gone out of sight. Sudhir has gone out of her life. He was bound to—after all, Tagar is not Vimla.

'Why did you throw him out?' Maanada asks.

Tagar quietly goes to her bed and lies down. The world was upturned in that fraction of a second. She does not feel unhappy, angry, or despondent. She feels a dull ache deep within. She lies lifelessly on her bed, reliving the past as memories flock by. From the forest faraway, piercing the earth it was buried in, the cry of a newborn baby chases her, tormenting her soul as it were.

The clouds are thundering out there.

In the next room, the two men from Kabul are exchanging raunchy jokes in an unintelligible tongue. How's Radha coping?

Shashi returns to the room. 'Won't you eat, Tagar?' he asks.

'Have you already eaten?'

'No, you eat first.'

Tagar is frozen in time.

Shashi sits down in the veranda and says, 'Don't brood over what happened in the past. That's the way of the world. You have already thought a lot more than you should about this worthless creature.'

'Stop this talk,' Tagar shoots back.

'All right,' Shashi replies with a wan smile. 'But do eat something…'

Tagar gets off the bed. She serves the rice she cooked in the morning and says, 'Here, have this.' As Shashi sits down to eat, Radha's agonized scream from the next room fills the air.

Tagar watches Shashi as he eats his dinner. A morsel fills his mouth and his right cheek bulges up. He looks happy and his wonderstruck eyes narrow with contentment.

Tagar experiences a deep affection coursing through her. Shashi loves her!

Tagar asks him, 'Hey, tell me, do you still love me?'

Shashi stops eating and gapes at her. His cow-like eyes are moist with a silent plea. After a pregnant pause he simply says, 'Won't you have your dinner now?'

Tagar settles down to her meal.

The storm raging outdoors has reached a crescendo as a fresh downpour sweeps the lane.

The men from Kabul chatter in an agitated voice as they walk down the stairs.

'Shashi, will you pour me some water?'

'Sure.'

Shashi washes his hand, pours water for Tagar, goes out to the veranda, puffs on a cigarette and stretches out.

'Why are you lying on the ground?'

'After all, this body too will turn into dust and merge with the earth one day,' Shashi jokes. 'Haven't you heard the Baul sing?'

'Merge with the earth? Don't yap! Get up, I'm telling you. Let me finish my dinner, then I will spread out a chattai and pillow for you.'

'All right.'

That's when they heard Maanada scream out: 'Oh god! Come running Boonchi, Tagar—Radha is finished!'

'What is she saying?' Tagar springs to her feet.

'You finish your dinner, I'll go and check what's the matter,' Shashi was already halfway to Radha's room.

What has happened to Radha? Tagar won't be able to eat until Shashi returns. She can hear Boonchi crying, 'Radha! Oh Radha, my sister—'

As if driven like a robot, Tagar reaches the door to Radha's room. She is lying unconscious on her dirty cot. But the duo from Kabul were not conmen, they have left a rupee near her head.

A crowd is jostling inside the room. The men are asking each other, creating a ruckus. Some are sprinkling water on Radha's face, some are fanning her.

The night is molten now.

A long time elapses before Tagar returns to her room. She goes on ruminating. It seems to her that the poison of guilt and hatred has insidiously spread through her body. She retches and passes out. Outside, the wind is lashing fiercely, the rains are pounding the earth. Just like her own life, the lane she lives in is fraught with inky darkness.

Shashi's heart melts when he returns to the room. He sprinkles water on Tagar and lulls her to sleep. 'Try and sleep, Tagar,' he tells her, 'it will set you right.'

'It will set everything right? Okay then,' Tagar closes her eyes. Again she starts to think—Vimla... the earth... 'you look familiar, who are you'... Memories have broken the dam of her mind. And then she remembers Radha's body that was devoid of blood or life...

Shashi clears the floor of her vomit, switches off the light, stretches out on the veranda again. The night is still getting drenched. The ceaseless downpour hasn't paused for a breath. The sky looks smeared with soot.

Suddenly Tagar jumps out of her bed. She switches on the light and calls out to Shashi. 'Shashi, oh Shashi!'

Tired, Shashi doesn't stir. Having slogged all through the day, he is in a deep slumber.

'Shashi, oh Shashi,' Tagar shakes him.

'Ooon…? Who's that?'

'It's me.'

'Who? Tagar?'

'Yes, Tagar.'

'What's the matter?'

'Let's go.'

'Where?'

'Just this evening you were telling me that you want to deliver me from this hell…'

Shashi's sleep-laden eyes show surprise. He gapes at Tagar in wonder. 'Is this a dream or reality?'

'Take me away from here, Shashi. Don't you love me?' Tagar's voice expresses the impatience of a distressed child.

Shashi's face changes in a split second. His dull eyes burn bright like embers. He holds Tagar by her arm and asks, 'Do you really mean what you are saying?'

Tagar clings to him like an innocent child and says, 'Yes, I really mean it, Shashi. Let's go right now. Don't dither or delay…'

Holding Tagar by her waist to help her stay on her feet, Shashi sweetly smiles. 'Come, let's march—'

The two of them set out of the lane.

'It's raining fiercely,' says Tagar.

'Yes. So what?'

'It's past midnight na, Shashi?' Tagar notices the darkness surrounding her.

'So what if it is pitch-dark? I will bring down the sun for you,' he responds, drawing her closer to himself.

The entire world is in slumber. It's raining incessantly. The sky is overcast with clouds, and there is no light on the horizon to melt the darkness. But there is no room for fear. The rains will stop, and dawn will break out, and people will wake up. And what will happen to Tagar and Shashi, the son of a prostitute? Their life will brighten up, for a new sun will usher a new day.

Translated from 'Woh Ek Raat' in
Chuninda Kahaniyaaan *by Padmaja Punde*

Anchor

Rustam Ali smiled. At last he could relax for a day or two. The anchor made a loud noise as it dropped into the water. Rahim and Keramat threw a thick rope over the jetty. On the port, Ganesh and Salim caught the rope and fastened it around a strong iron pole. For the last time, the ship's wheels rotated through the muddy waters of the river Padma. For the last time, the whistle thundered through the air like the roar of a demon. The sound urged the birds in the surrounding bushes and trees to call out and take flight. As the sound of the whistle died down, the flocks returned to their usual spots on the treetops. The goods carrier ship, *SS Ratna*, stopped at the harbour in Mirpur.

The daily passenger ship had docked early that morning and left twenty minutes later. Then, for seven or eight hours, the harbour remained quiet. Occasionally, the silence was interrupted by the loud voices of coolies, the station master and the goods clerk. Other than that, the ghats were lively with the sounds of women and children bathing, the Padma's lapping waters, cawing crows and calls of kites. But there was no sense of busyness or hurry. Instead, a feel of continuity and idyllic beauty seemed to envelope the landscape. Then again, the harbour grew busy as *SS Ratna* docked. The vehicle's heartbeat seemed to come to a slow halt. It started swaying with the waves of the river. The station master, Hosain Miya, climbed the pontoon bridge and came to the ship. Behind him was the goods clerk, Haridas Mittir.

The captain of the ship was Mr Thomas. A sahib, but not Western, an Indian—special resident of Chattagram (Chittagong). No one knew whether he had a family. He never spoke of them. But while cleaning his room, Rustam Ali and Anaya Khalasi had seen a picture of a sad-looking young lady in a frock near a vase with paper flowers on his tabletop. She was not an Indian but of mixed origin. The people on the ship guessed that he had some connection with that lady. Sareng Yakub Miya believed that the captain liked the girl, but he could not win her as she was stone-hearted. No one disbelieved Yakub Miya. He was aged, he prayed four times a day; his piousness and age had whitened his beard. Other than that, on several nights, had the crew not seen the captain, high on whisky, gaze longingly at the picture? Had they not seen the drunken captain murmur and weep and grind his teeth in front of the photograph? Not just that, the crew had seen him drunk, swearing, but never had they seen their sahib express any weakness for women. He had extraordinary resilience when it came to women, absolutely amazing.

Captain Thomas was coming down the stairs.

Hosain Miya saluted the captain with a smile, 'Good morning, Mr Thomas! Meeting after ages, what do you say?'

Mr Thomas nodded in assent, 'Yes, coming after three months. Good morning,' he added.

The goods clerk said, 'Very glad to see you sir—welcome.'

Mr Thomas put his hands in his pocket and stood upright. 'Do not avoid duty, Mr Miya. What goods do you have for us?'

'All jute, sahib—three thousand mounds.'

'Hmm. That means three days—we will have to stay three days.'

The goods clerk laughed like a jackal and batted his eyelids. 'He-hey... Fate sir, fate—absent for three months, therefore stay for three days—he-hey.'

Mr Thomas did not react to the goods clerk's attempt at humour. He merely frowned and glanced menacingly. The goods clerk's laughter froze in his throat.

Hosain Miya assessed the situation and quickly said, 'Take rest, Captain. Chicken, eggs and fish are very cheap here.'

Rustam Ali stretched his muscular arms and said, 'Oh, saved! Three days to rest and relax.'

Rahim winked and laughed, 'You are right! We can have fun after dusk!'

Keramat shook his head, 'But for one thing...'

'What?'

'Is that oldie Badshah Miya still alive? Last time he almost collapsed one evening.'

Rustam smiled, 'Why would he not be alive? Do the children of the devil die early? The old man will surely be alive.'

'Bastards, what is happening here?' Mr Thomas came and stood in front of them. He laughed cruelly, baring his big, flashy teeth.

Rustam replied with a weak smile, 'We were just chatting, huzoor.'

'Shut up!' Thomas thundered. 'Don't talk nonsense, swines—go wash the decks and clean up!'

'Yes huzoor, we are going.' The three friends ran from there.

Thomas gave a short laugh, 'Bloody swines...the whole lot of them!'

Hidden from the captain, Rustam burst out, 'Son of a bastard! Bastard's son bastard! Heathen!'

Rahim and Keramat covered their mouths and chuckled.

All the meals were over. It was an autumn evening. The river looked scary. When the mild breeze started blowing in the evening, the sparse vegetation on the banks receded behind a haze. The waves of the demonic Padma roared like a dragon. Pushed by the giant waves, *SS Ratna* started swaying. The jetty and the towboats also swayed. Mr Thomas started pacing the deck like a lone gorilla. Whenever strong winds blew on the river, Mr Thomas's appearance altered. The disturbed state of nature gave voice to his own internal disturbance.

Work had started on the ghats. The coolies were loading bundles of jute from the godowns to the waiting towboats. The goods clerk supervised the activity from behind his nickel-framed glasses. With him were two persons: a jotedar, a powerful landowner, and a mahajan, the local moneylender. Old Sareng Yakub Miya sat singing a lovelorn ghazal. His voice was coarse but he still sang.

Rustam joked, 'I can see that the old uncle still has many yearnings!'

'Why will I not, you owl?' Yakub Mia retorted. 'Am I beyond Khuda Tala's world?'

Rustam said in a low voice, 'Then come with us tonight.'

'Where?' Old Sareng pretended not to understand.

'A little colour and drama.'

'Tauba, tauba!' Yakub Miya bit his tongue, 'Are you my saala or my nephew, Rustam?'

'Don't be cross, uncle!'

'Don't be cross?' Yakub Miya bared his teeth. 'Why not, Rustam? Have you ever noticed how old you are?'

Rustam sobered down. Any mention of his age always shut him up. His whole past seemed to burn through him like a flame and turned his body and soul into ash.

He skulked away silently.

'Hey Rustam,' Yakub Miya called out after him, 'listen—are you angry?'

Rustam made no reply. He held on to the railings and gazed at the ghats. Some veiled girls were bathing in the river. The force of the waves lifted them like lotus stems. The evening sun sporting the colour of an orange had descended behind the foliage of Mirpur. The strong wind prodded the waves of the Padma to noisily hit the banks. The trees swirled. All said, the atmosphere was pensive. The heart longed for something. What did it desire? How old was he? Nearing forty. Seven years ago—let that be. He was not too aged. Forty was not 'old'. He had no regret about his age. That never saddened him. He felt morose because his past depressed him. Forget that story...

The veiled faces of the bathing women were not visible. All at once Rustam longed to see their faces. The women in the river were like the river itself—deep, dangerous and life-giving. Rustam really fancied the water that swayed, the soft earth, greenery, the blue skies—and women. Very beautiful.

Suddenly, one of the girl's veil shifted a little. Just for a second—like the lightning. She was probably twenty-seven years old but she looked tender, very soft and young. Rustam felt a twinge of sadness. There was a time when a certain woman stood by him in such surroundings, he would touch her, whisper endearments... Let that be. It was better the bones remained concealed in the grave.

Thirst. An unquenchable, infinite thirst. Desire.

Rustam swiftly moved away from there. He went and joined Rahim and Keramat who were sitting in a corner smoking bidis.

Rahim teased him, 'What happened friend? You look troubled!'

'No more jokes,' Rustam said. 'Let's go.'

'Where?'

'Let's look for Badshah Miya in Shahbuddin's Hotel.'

'The bastard sahib will notice.'

'He won't notice. Let's go.'

Dressed in clean lungis and half-sleeved shirts, and tucking in knives along with colourful leather wallets, the three left surreptitiously. They only informed Yakub Miya. The old man did not object.

But they did not expect what happened. How could they have imagined that the captain of the ship would be scanning the area with his binoculars? They had just crossed the pontoon when his thundering voice demanded, 'Hey—where are you going—you bloody swines?'

The three quietly returned, grinding their teeth like wild animals.

'Where were you making off? Why are you running, you thieves—to which hell?'

Rustam raised his voice to say, 'We were going into town huzoor, to look around.'

Thomas guffawed showing his shiny teeth. 'Going for a stroll, huh? You blasted liars—can't you speak the truth?'

'We are speaking the truth.'

'Oh!' The captain laughed again. 'Why not admit that you are going for wine and women, huh?' Suddenly he thundered,

'Scamper, you ponies. But if you are not back by 9 p.m., I will give you hell. Now go—run—'

Rustam reached the jetty in silence and then swore at the captain, 'Idiot, son of a monkey! By god, one day I will spit on his face!'

Behind the port were two sweet shops and pice hotels—one catered to Hindus, the other to Muslims. Next to those were small kiosks selling paan, bidi and cigarette. Then after a barren stretch were shops selling clothes, grocery, jewellery, a post office, a registry office—the area was brimming with activity and crowds.

Shahabuddin's hotel was fairly crowded. Another ship was to dock that evening, so people from the surrounding villages had gathered. Most of the travellers were headed for Goalundo. They were already eating and drinking—most of them wanted to finish all that before the ship docked.

Rustam entered Shahabuddin's hotel with his friends.

In a machan made of bamboo, Shahabuddin was chewing paan and conversing with the travellers. He saw Rustam and greeted him, 'Welcome. Do come in bhai saheb…'

'Salaam walekum, saab.'

'Walekum salaam. Walekum salaam.'

Rustam laughed, 'How are you, miya sahib? All well?'

Shahabuddin could not place them. He half closed his eyes, and in a Gabriel-like voice, he sweetly said, 'But janab—where have I seen you?'

Rahim shook his head, 'I'm not surprised that you don't recognize us, miyajaan—our ship was here three months ago.'

Shahabuddin fingered the end of his beard and laughed. 'Now I recognize you, friend,' he said. 'Sit. Sit and rest.'

Suddenly Rustam heard an effeminate voice address him, 'How are you, Sohrab's father? All well?'

Instantly Rustam turned his head. All three friends jumped to their feet.

'Badshah Miya!'

'Shahenshah Miya!'

'Salaam walekum.'

'Walekum salaam.'

'We were looking for you, miyajaan.'

'Oh?'

'Yes diler.'

'Why, dear musafir?'

'Come. Come have a bidi.'

Their antics made Shahabuddin laugh as he stroked the strands of his beard. The three friends had encircled Badshah Miya. It seemed they had been friends for more than twenty years—hard to believe that they had met only for a day three months ago.

Sitting amidst the trio Badshah Miya smiled to himself. For a sixty-year-old, he combed his beard and whiskers well. He was a skinny man with small eyes. He wore a patched lungi and a collarless fatua. The gamchha on his shoulder was worn out but sparkling clean. He sure had taste. Life had fulfilled none of his desires, and that was probably why his zest for living had not died.

Old Badshah seemed to be overflowing with ardour. Revealing wide gaps between paan-stained teeth, the gentleman said, 'I say, what is it? Why are you pampering me, youngsters?'

Rustam spoke in a pleading tone, 'For a favour, grandpa.'

Badshah Miya smiled, 'That means?'

'Do not pretend, miyajaan! Tonight you must introduce us to houris and fairies—get it?'

'Huh! I should introduce you? Then you will have to wait for some days.'

'Why? Why?'

'First, I must go to heaven.'

'You talk nonsense, granddad,' Keramat retorted. 'You already live in heaven!'

Rahim added, 'You can do everything, miyajaan.'

Rustam touched the bottom of Badshah Miya's silvery beard, kissed his fingers, clicked his tongue and said, 'You are a magician, grandpa. You have Aladdin's lamp.'

Badshah Miya shook his head like a lizard. 'Then listen to me—' he said.

'Yes yes.'

'Moonlike face, cloud-like hair—'

'Oh! Oh! Oh!'

'Eyebrows arched like wings of a falcon—'

'Right.'

'And lips luscious with the juice of pomegranate—'

'No doubt.'

'Basra roses on her cheeks—'

'Wow!'

'And like moong dal, she is golden.'

'Oh! We will die for her!'

Badshah Miya lowered his head and uttered playfully, 'Do you want?'

Rustam stood up in excitement and lifted Badshah Miya. The old man looked like a frightened rat and yelped. 'Put me down, miya, put me down,' he demanded, laughing loud. 'Don't tease me—otherwise, I will insult your forefathers through fourteen generations—'

Shahabuddin's hotel was filled with the boisterous laughter of the friends. He said, 'Such laughter on an empty stomach? What will happen after you finish a bottle?'

Rustam swung his thumb and said, 'Goose egg—sheer nothing!'

The evening passed. It was dusk. A sliver of moon climbed atop the coconut trees. The passengers got off and onto the steamer on time. The sounds of crickets and jackals announced it was night.

The travellers to Goalondo had all left. Four or five more crew members of the ship descended upon the hotel, as did hooligans from the village. Young, old, everyone. Then, there was not only fish, mutton, kebab and rice, there was country liquor as well. The room was filled with smoke from Scissors cigarettes and bidis. In one corner, by the light of gas lanterns, Rustam and his friends were shuffling cards, chewing meat off bones and downing liquor. Slowly, they were getting drunk. But, except Rustam Ali, the rest were sozzled.

Rustam had not lost his senses. His gaze was fixed on the door for Badshah Miya. The old man had left more than an hour ago and would return after he had fixed everything.

Rustam was getting impatient. It was after nightfall. If it got too late in the night, things would get difficult. Their captain was a rigid man; he would behave like a wild animal if they were too late. Everyone would be in trouble.

Gambling had started in another corner. Rahim and Keramat were hollering there. 'Hey! We will also play—'

'We will woo back lady luck—huh—'

'Show me the money.'

One could hear the jingling of coins. Rustam just sat and waited. It was as if an unseen flame consumed him from within.

Suddenly he heard Badshah Miya's effeminate voice whispering to him, 'Ei shipmate, come out fast—quick—'

Instantly all his senses were roused, like a tiger on the prowl.

It was as if Badshah Miya was riding a strong breeze. The sliver of moon had disappeared. The darkness had deepened. The roads could no more be seen. Badshah Miya was walking through the jungle behind the hotel. Rustam was following him.

'How much further is it, miyajaan? '

'Don't panic steamboat—here we are—'

They clamoured on to a village path. Badshah Miya stepped a few paces forward and said to Rustam, 'Wait.'

Rustam stopped. An unusual sensation coursed through his body making him stiff. Darkness, solitariness, the call of crickets—overriding all of these was his longing for a woman. He did not even know how she looked.

Badshah Miya called out softly, 'Fatima—oh Fatima!'

In the darkness a spirit-like figure was materializing at a distance. As the apparition drew near, it became a woman.

Badshah Miya patted Rustam and said softly, 'Here is your houri—now go, miya.'

'Where should I go?'

'Where else but her home? The night will be spoilt in this den of snakes—'

'Okay.' Rustam took out a matchbox from his pocket. He lit a matchstick and held it in front of the woman.

For just a moment. It was as if a streak of lightning had revealed an ethereal face to Rustam. It looked familiar with its longish shape, large eyes, luscious lips, shy and magical veneer. Where had he seen her?

'So then, let me go ahead. Old man—what do you say?'

Badshah Miya held back Rustam by his hand and said, 'Yes, you will go but first pay me for my labours.'

'How much?'

'One rupee.'

'My God!'

'People call God when they want to live.'

'And if I don't give?'

Badshah Miya's voice turned harsh as he said, 'I am a magician, I will make this houri vanish before your very eyes.'

'Here's your rupee.'

Like a hungry python, the old man's right hand swooped on Rustam's palm and snatched the money.

'And what happens to Rahim and Keramat?' Rustam wanted to know.

Suddenly Badshah Miya's effeminate voice was laced with masculine sternness. 'Don't worry about them, sahib,' he said. 'There is no dearth of starving women in this country.'

'Seriously?'

'In actual fact. Unable to survive, many of them have staked their honour for a meal. But will times always remain the same, miya? Man is not just an animal—'

'What are you saying, miya? What do you mean?'

'Man can forget every slight but never the affront of having to sell his honour. That is why the ones who bow to your lusty breath today will turn around and behead you tomorrow.'

Rustam put his hand on the dagger buried in his waistband and stood up straight. 'Old man, you are putting me off,' he said. 'I swear to khuda…'

'Enjoy yourself,' Badshah Miya cut him short, 'I am off.' He cackled like a frog and melted into the darkness.

Stunned.

By and by Rustam inched towards the girl. She was standing still at that spot but took two steps back when Rustam moved forward. He strode forward, grabbed her hand and drew her to his chest. The girl pushed him away with both her hands but cooed, 'Please come home.'

Rustam was moved by her softness. With a drunken smile he slurred, 'Let's go, bibijaan.'

The girl walked ahead and Rustam followed her. Both sides of the path were flanked by a thick overgrowth of vegetation. The air vibrated with the call of crickets, the darkness stretched uninterrupted, the ground was damp with dewdrops. All of this infused the mood with a sense of mystery and adventure. Rustam again fingered the dagger hidden in his clothings. There was no saying what could happen; one could not trust anyone. It was best to be prepared.

The house had a thatched roof. There was no other house for about two hundred yards. It was a worn-out shelter that might give way the next monsoon. The patch of land surrounding the house was an extension of the jungle. At the back was a ditch which gave off the stench of rotten vegetation that cut through the air every now and then.

The girl opened the chain that locked the door. Her soft voice said, 'Come in.'

Rustam entered the room.

It was a single bedroom. The flickering lamp fed by redi oil had filled the room with the smell of its burnt wick. Rustam looked around. The harshness of poverty had left the room bare. A five- or six-year-old boy was soundly asleep on an unsteady bed. Pale and emaciated, he lay in a posture that revealed his exhaustion.

The girl stepped out of the room into the inner courtyard. Rustam went and stood next to her.

Silence.

Rustam suddenly found time hanging heavy on his hands. The cricket's call hung in the air. The bark of a dog drifted from the distant habitation. Some bird sleeping on the trees fluttered its wings. Night. An unknown village, filled with echoes of entrancement. At hand was an unknown woman. It felt strange. Unusual. An unpleasant adventure. But what was the solution? The roots of his life had shrivelled. His past had been washed away and cleansed in that one night. He had drowned it before he set sail in the ocean. He had no home, no household to call his own. There was no woman who could pluck the strings of his heart. Other than that, he had grown in years. Even if it disheartened him, it was a reality. Therefore, this was better. His life had become one with the ship. Now and then he would spend a day or two relaxing at a port, familiar or unknown. In the process he would gain some experiences. In any case, how many days of his life were left? The time to lie in a grave was drawing nearer.

Grave! He hated to think of it. One day he would have to leave behind this tempting life and the wide world. Rustam instantaneously snapped out of the thought. What was he thinking? What would be would be—why must he think of it now? This was the time to quench his yearning.

He pulled the girl towards him and said, 'Why aren't you asking me to sit?'

Again she pushed him away and took two steps back. Then she took out a torn rug and spread it out in the courtyard. 'Sit,' she said to him.

Rustam did not sit. He said, 'Get the lamp.'

'Why?'

'I want to see you.'

'I am not worth looking at, miya sahib.'

Astonishing voice. It stirred his passion with its calmness. Impassive yet pleasing, the dying embers of lust were suddenly inflamed. Rustam felt the blood rush to his head as he stood close to the woman's body. He went inside and fetched the lamp. When he held it before the girl, its magical light showed a longish face with sad, drooping eyes and a luscious pout. Dark complexioned. She wore no jewellery, only some glass bangles. Still, she was arresting, very unusual.

'Your name?'

'Fatima.'

'Fatima!' Rustam put down the lamp and smiled. 'Lovely. Beautiful name—you look beautiful too.'

The girl did not move. Her face expressed no emotion. Girls normally like to be praised for their beauty, but in this case? She stayed inscrutable like a stone statuette. Only her eyes glowed like glass. Where was the sparkle of life?

The face looked familiar. He seemed to have seen her somewhere. Today at the port. But, nowhere else? As he tried to place her, he got a shock. It was not Fatima, but thirteen years ago her clone had come into his life. Amina. Her complexion, countenance, contours—none of these were like Fatima. But there was a strange similarity between the two.

It was as if in that dim light, Rustam's whole past rose before him like a drowned ship rising out of water. In distant Chattagram, in a tiny house lived his old mother and Amina. He had around five bighas of land. He tilled his land and worked as a labourer in a farm. Despite scarcity, poverty, disorder and bareness, they still had golden crops. The soil and Amina—day and night's magical stories. But one day the devil cast his shadow on earth. War. Fire. The market was aflame. His mother died. Scarcity came and grabbed his open palm. He took loans from the mahajan. Soon the moneylender complained that the loan was not getting repaid. His land went. He felt as if half his life had gone. Then? Then came the famine. There was no food in the house. Rustam went to town. The God of War swayed the world—a phantom-like Rustam roamed the streets of the ghost town for days on end. Hunger. He roamed like a hungry dog. One day he found employment with a contractor. Other than food, he was paid ten rupees. He worked for a few days, took an advance of five rupees and sent it to his village. After ten days the money came back to him. Amina was not in the village. Where had she gone? Rustam went mad. He left his job and fled at night. He walked and walked and reached his village in the wee hours of the morning. He went home and called out to Amina. There was no answer. By the light of the moon in the sky he could see the door was slightly ajar. He went forward. Suddenly the putrid smell of rotting human flesh choked him. He pushed the door and entered, covering his nose with a cloth. The door creaked. In the moonlight entering the room he could see someone lying on the floor, wearing Amina's old paachha-paar sari. The person on the floor was not living but dead. The jackals had bitten off and eaten from the body—her face, bust, more. It was difficult to identify the body but there was no mistake. The torn sari, the bangles and the curly hair proclaimed her identity.

Rustam's screams had rent the village at dawn but not a sound came in return. Most villagers had fled. Like one possessed,

Rustam went and sat outside the room. He did not find the smell of rotten flesh nauseating any more. A long time passed. The sun came up. He dug up the courtyard and buried Amina's remains. Then he left the village.

When did this happen? Almost six years ago. For six years, Rustam had tied his life to the wheels of the ship. At first he would feel sad. He would stay by himself. But when he was alone, he was scared. Amina's ghastly, disfigured body seemed to chase him. To run away from that, one day he buried his past in women and wine. Anyway, let his past go to hell—why should he dwell on it and ruin the rest of his life?

But today he was reminiscing again. Not the distorted body but the living Amina's face. Her words. Her manners. On a romantic night, the embrace of two young arms, two seeking lips, and the sweet murmur of romance. Fatima seemed to resemble that Amina.

What nonsense was he reminiscing! He must have been very drunk. Well, he could enjoy himself again. Fatima was beautiful.

'Fatima—'

She did not reply.

'Come here.'

Fatima did not move.

'Do you hear me?'

Now she moved her lips. She spoke with the same soft voice, 'I can hear. Can I have the money first?'

'Sure. But if I don't give?'

No answer.

Rustam laughed loudly. 'Okay bibi, don't be angry with me,' he guffawed. 'Here, take your money. How much should I give you? One rupee…here, take two rupees.' He took out two rupees from his pocket and put it on the torn rug. Then he went to drag Fatima onto the rug.

Fatima picked up the cash and said, 'Wait, I will just come—'

'Don't delay, bibi. The bastard will lose his intoxication.'

Fatima went inside.

Time passed. Fatima did not return. What was the matter? Rustam got up.

'Where are you, Fatima bibi?'

'Here,' a grim voice sounded behind him.

Rustam turned around. Fatima stood on the doorway with a scythe—and fire in her eyes.

'Hey what kind of a game is this, bibi?'

'Now you get out, miya—'

'Oh! I see, so you are a woman gangster!' Rustam laughed out loud.

'Will you leave or not mister? The consequences will not be good.'

Rustam dragged fear onto his visage and said, 'Of course I will leave, bibi. Here I go.'

He moved towards the door. Then swiftly he swung back. Within moments the table turned. He jumped on Fatima. There was a faint shriek. The heartless tigress made a last attempt but she could not manage. Rustam took the scythe from her hand and threw it at a distance.

Then he took out the dagger from his belt and laughed. 'Now, Fatima bibi?' he chewed out.

Again the girl turned to stone. Rustam pulled her to him with one arm, held her in close embrace and drew her face to his.

Abruptly he stopped. Fatima was shivering, shivering hard. Her tremulous eyes were filled with fear and tears. The teardrops flowed down her cheeks. Her lips were quivering. She started crying.

Maybe she was pretending, maybe cheating, faking. Still it felt awkward. Rustam's heart that had hardened like a demon's, seemed to soften—he let Fatima go. Fatima flopped to the floor.

His intoxication had passed. Something like this had never happened to him. He could not picture anything like this. For years he had not seen a young woman weep in front of him. After ages, his heart seemed to have lightened, as if the stone that lay on it had been lifted.

He put back the dagger in his waistband and sat down facing Fatima.

'Fatima—'

Her tears had not ebbed.

'Why are you crying?'

Fatima turned her face away, 'Out of sorrow.'

'What sorrow?'

'This is the first time in my life—'

'It is not my fault, bibi.'

'No—the fault is mine. Not a single paisa in hand. The child has not eaten a morsel for two days. Badshah Miya scolded me one day when I went to pick up unhusked rice. He said he could not give me the rice but I had youth and if I swallowed my self-respect, I would not lack for food. Today when I saw my son's suffering, I recalled what he had said. That is why I saw him this evening and told him I was available. Then—'

'Hmm. Who do you have besides your son?'

'No one.'

'When did your husband die?'

'Two years ago.'

'What had happened to him?'

'Nothing. The landlord killed him. Not with his own hand, by goondas.'

'Why?'

'He was the head of the farmers.'

'How do you manage now?'

'I cannot manage.'

'Did you not have land or property?'

'We had. But the mahajan took it over as we could not repay his loans. We only have this shelter. This too will probably go to the moneylender—he is after it.'

'I see. Why? Is the loan not yet repaid?'

'No.' For the first time, a smile played on Fatima's lips. A stunning smile. She continued, 'The mahajan is willing to let go. And he wants to give me an allowance of five-ten rupees a month.'

'Why? Pity?'

'No. My honour. The moneylender lusts for it.'

Moneylender! Moneylender! Rustam's head was throbbing.

Softly he asked, 'What is his name?'

'Tayeb Ali Sheikh.'

'Where does he live?'

'Close to the township.'

'Hmm.'

Rustam took out two more rupees, put them on the floor and stood up. 'Do not be scared of me, bibi,' he said to Fatima. 'Keep this money and feed your son. I am a sailor—I have an uncertain existence—but at one time, I also had everything. Okay, I will be off. It is late. I no longer have any urges. And my captain is a real bastard.' Rustam completed his statement and looked at Fatima.

Fatima sat still leaning against the wall. She did not utter a sound. She only cast a silent glance at Rustam and then turned her face away.

The sun lay immersed in the river Padma. Now through the mild haze on the river the fiery ball slowly raised its head. Its crimson light made the river look glorious, divine. It was a new dawn.

Rustam was not supposed to wake up then. He had returned quite late. When the ship docked at a port, Rustam slept better. Today also he was asleep.

Suddenly Mr Thomas said, 'Hey—son of a bitch—hey!'

An astounded Rustam scrambled to his feet.

Thomas screamed like a wild boar, 'When did you return last night, you son of a bitch!'

'At the right time, huzoor.'

'What? You are lying, bastard!'

'It was only a wee bit late.'

'But why—where did you go? You are all dirty profligates—you should be whipped.'

The half-asleep Rustam did not respond. He knew the sahib well.

'Listen, you cannot go out today.'

'All right, sir.'

'Now go. Go clean the deck—alone.'

Peace.

Rustam gnashed his teeth and muttered, 'Bastard—owl—son of an owl—'

As soon as the captain left, Rahim and Keramat came out of hiding. They twirled around Rustam like dancers and said, 'Now go clean the deck.'

Old Sareng came and stood there chuckling. He stroked his beard and said, 'Your day will go well, Rustam. Have you seen sahib's face?'

Rahim asked, 'Tell me, which heaven were you in yesterday? You left us behind and had all the fun by yourself? What sort of a friend are you?'

Rustam smiled a benign smile, 'You are making up stories.' Keramat pretended to scold him, 'Now go bloody swine—hold your ears and do sit-ups.'

Rustam did not respond. He was thinking of the previous night. The events seemed unreal in daylight. It felt like he had dreamt up the whole experience. But it certainly was not that. He clearly remembered the girl's face. No, it was not a dream. How could he forget someone who reminded him of Amina?

The early morning passenger ferry came into view.

The morning had pressed the 'Start' button of the daily routine. Only, the wheels of the ship were not rotating. Still, there was a lot of work. The deck had to be washed and cleaned. The instruments needed to be oiled. Food had to be cooked. Time kept ticking by.

Every now and then, Thomas's angry shouts punctuated the air like the barking of a mad dog. Thomas was always in a bad temper when the ship was still.

On the other bank of the vast Padma was a line of forest cover. As the sun rose higher in the sky, the bank faded from view. A distant sound of melee wafted in from the market. Many banana boats and fishing boats had docked along the ghat. Men, women, old folks and kids were bathing in the water. The voices of Hosain Miya and the goods clerk could be heard above the din, calling out instructions to the coolies loading the jute onto the tugboats that would ferry them to the ship. The fetid smell of jute pervaded the air. The day grew older. The sun got hotter. The breeze blew stronger. The river changed colour. *SS Ratna* kept swaying, and so did Rustam Ali's mind.

Every now and then Rustam seemed to be seeking someone among the bathers. No, she was not there. At times Rustam Ali was distracted. A pair of large eyes seemed to float into his vision repeatedly. The face that reminded him of Amina. Where has that life gone? Home, field, wife and household? The moneylender! The poor everywhere lived through the same story. His life and Fatima's life seemed the same. He lost his wife; Fatima lost her husband. It was the same cycle. Khuda Tala was not responsible, humans were. It has been so forever.

The afternoon rolled by, evening approached, the sun grew orange again. And Rustam grew impatient. His legs had become like those of a race horse—raring to get off the ship. His forehead was crisscrossed with frown lines.

As soon as dusk set in, he went to Rahim and said, 'Come mate, let us go for a walk.'

Rahim laughed, 'How will you evade Thomas's searchlight eyes?'

'By God I will do it. Just join me.'

An hour and half later.

Fatima was shocked to see Rustam at her doorstep.

'You!'

'Yes—but do not fear, Fatima bibi. I have no ulterior motive.'

Fatima was astounded to see Rustam. His hair was dishevelled. On the right side of his forehead was a red weltering wound, his lower lip was cut, swollen. How?

'What happened to you, miya sahib?'

Rustam laughed it off, 'Oh nothing! I just had a fight.'

'With whom?'

'With…what was his name? Yes yes, Tayeb Ali Sheikh.'

Fatima's eyeballs were suddenly glowing. 'Why?' she asked. 'Why did you fight with Tayeb Ali?'

'Just like that. I do not like jotedars and mahajans. Landowners and moneylenders—they raise my fury. Besides, that swine is the one who has pushed you on the path of ruin. Bloody bastard! But bibi, won't you ask me to sit even today?'

With a melancholic smile, Fatima welcomed him, 'Please come in. Take a seat.'

'You are not scared, are you?'

'You asked me not to be afraid!'

Rustam smiled and entered the tenement. Fatima's son sat on the bed, scribbling on a broken slate. When he saw an unknown face, he locked his arms and sat still.

Rustam went to him and ran an affectionate hand on his head, 'Little boy, what is your name?'

The boy answered, 'Akbar Ali.'

'Really? You have a nice name, son.'

Silence.

Fatima said, 'I see you have a nasty cut—wait.'

Fatima returned with a wet rag and said, 'Let me clean your wound.'

Rustam shut his eyes and let her clean his wound. Then he opened his eyes and said, 'My life is just like yours, Fatima bibi.'

Fatima looked at him sharply. 'How?' she asked.

'You and I have a lot in common. I work on a ship now but once I also had fields, farm, a home and a household. Gone. Now all that is gone. Your husband was murdered, my wife was food for jackals and dogs…'

Fatima took two steps toward Rustam, 'How?'

'Famine.'

A discomfiting silence descended in the room. Painful, palpable. The boy climbed down from the bed and clung to his mother. Rustam looked at them. The crickets had started their evening raga. A cool breeze murmured through the woods. A small room, a clay lamp, dim light, the cowdung-plastered floor, the smell of wet earth, one woman, one child—it was tempting. A fierce desire wrenched his heart. His past floated up like a sunken ship might. Six years had gone by. For six years, his life had been unthinking, reckless, chaotic. All these days he had tried to fill up the vacuum in his life with wine, women and partying. But today he felt a longing for a home, a land to plough and reap gold at harvest time.

'Fatima bibi—'

Fatima looked at him.

'Why don't you marry again? How long will you battle on alone like this?'

'How long? I don't know. Who will marry me? Everybody is badly off in the village. Everyone wants me only for a day. For one night. This very afternoon the mahajan was here. He threatened me: if I do not give in to him in another seven days, he will drive us away from this shelter of our ancestors.'

'Fatima bibi...'

'Yes, please.'

'There are many in this world who will want a nikah with you.'

Stillness again.

Rustam stood up. He hesitated a while, then went on, 'Achha bibi sahib, am I a very bad man?'

Fatima smiled. She looked at Rustam and said, 'How can I judge in one day?'

'Hmm. Okay—goodbye.'

Quickly he left the room, as if he was running away,

He cursed himself as he left. What nonsense had he spoken? He was a sailor. The ship was his home and the river his world. How could he think of a home, a household, field and farming?

After half an hour.

The inspector bid farewell. Mr Thomas said, 'Good night, inspector—don't worry, I shall give them a good lesson. I will fire the rascals after this trip.'

The inspector shook his head in assent, 'Yes. Do that. I am releasing them only because of you. It is not a light offence to beat up a respectable jotedar. They almost killed him. If we put them on trial, they would be jailed for two-three years.'

Thomas politely replied, 'Thank you, inspector sahib. I will be forever grateful to you.'

'Good night.'

The inspector left with the constables. In a flash Thomas turned fierce. He strode down the stairs and showed up in the lower deck.

'Where? Where is that rascal?' His thundering voice surprised the crew.

'Where is the dog—Rustam Ali?'

Rustam had returned barely five minutes before this. He had heard every word about Tayeb Ali's complaint, how the police had been bribed to come and arrest him from the ship. The agitated crew were abusing him and Rahim. It was exactly at this moment that Thomas roared, 'Rustam Ali!'

Rustam took his time to stand before Thomas. His forehead and lips bore the signs of the brawl, so there was no question of denying it. He did not open his mouth.

'Here—you hooligan, badmash, shaitan—but why? Why did you fight?'

'The moneylender abused me, sir.'

'You are a liar.'

'No, sir.'

'But why would he abuse you without a reason?'

'He did that, huzoor.'

'Hmm. And who were with you?'

'No one, sir. Only some villagers.'

'Tell me exactly, who were there?'

'No one, sir.'

Thomas laughed showing his teeth. He said, 'Swine—you are a scoundrel. But listen—if this ever happens again, I shall kick you off the ship. I will throw you out.'

Thomas started to leave. Then he turned back. 'Listen,' he said, 'listen carefully all of you—the jute has been loaded. We will set out tomorrow at ten in the morning.'

The ship got busy at dawn. At seven, it was sparkling clean. Rustam and Rahim loaded coal on the boiler. Everything was fine.

Hosain Miya and the goods clerk were busy. The morning passenger ferry docked and left. Then the receipts for 3000 mounds of jute were signed. The clock swung from seven to eight, then from eight to nine.

The trees lining the opposite bank could still be seen. The sky was blue. The terns were soaring near the ghats. The coolies were shouting. The sailors on the banana boats were talking to those rowing the fishermen's boats. You could hear the soft lapping of the waters of the Padma.

A pair of large sad eyes, a longish face, luscious lips, skin glowing like a newborn leaf—as Rustam kept thinking, he was getting distracted. The girl looked like Amina. There was no Amina, no home, no family, no peace. Amina's rotten, half-eaten body lay in a grave. Amina was not buried. She lived. In his heart. In his memories. In the glances and smiles of all women. In their soft touch and in their love. But Rustam had no choice. Doomsday waters had submerged the port of his life.

One side of the ghat was crowded by bathers. You could hear the voices of children. Rustam looked carefully. No. That face was not there. His heart felt leaden. It would have been good to see the girl.

Thomas was blaring, 'Hey Sareng, where are you? Looks like the aged bastard cannot work—'

On the other side Rahim was humming a song:

Oh gifted woman, do not cast me away
I have given my heart to you—

Rustam stopped to listen. Rahim sang well.

The ship blew its first whistle. It was a long siren. It was as if *SS Ratna* was bidding farewell to every soul in the haven at Mirpur.

'Hoiii—throw the rope ji—'

The tow boat was attached to the ship. The stench of jute filled the air. The engine had come alive. An impatient stream of steam seemed to wrap itself around the ship letting out a long wail: *po—u-u-u-uu.*

This time he had had an eventful stay in the port of Mirpur.

Rustam dwelt on the night before. And the previous night. The girl's life seemed like a mirror image of his life. They were both like broken ships. But was there nobody to love? When a storm assails a huge expanse of water, does it put an end to the romance of journey?

'Hoiii—ring the bell ji.'

The machinery started rolling. The second whistle of the ship had sounded. Hosain Miya and the goods clerk came to see off the captain.

'Good bye captain, come again—chicken and fish is really cheap here.'

By this time the motion of the ship was flowing in the veins of Mr Thomas, his mind had spread its wings for distant horizons. He smiled unmindfully, 'Yes yes. Goodbye, miya sahib.'

Rustam stood looking around. No, there was no sign of those drooping eyes on the ghats.

Hosain Miya and the goods clerk left.

Suddenly Thomas noticed Rustam. 'What are you doing here,' he barked, 'standing idle and silent? Go, go start work!'

Rustam moved off from his post.

'Hoiii—pull ji.' The anchor rose up from the chest of the river. The coolies of the port started to pull the pontoon away.

Another whistle.

The wheels of the ship churned the waters of the Padma. The ship rocked. Then it started to move away from the banks.

Rustam climbed down to the deck below. He went and stood at the back of the ship. The port of Mirpur was receding slowly. Again, only water, then a few ports with taverns, wine and paid women to cheat life. No. There was no hope. Home, family, wife, kids, bullocks, ploughs—these had gone out of his life for good.

But was that true? Was there no tomorrow?

Rustam suddenly swung himself onto the rope that was tied to the tow boat. He swung in the air and then put his foot on the tow boat. He took care to hide himself as he skirted around the tugboat. Then he plunged into the water.

At first Rustam seemed to go under the water that fumed with the churning of the ship's wheels. But that was for seconds. The next minute he floated up to see *SS Ratna* leave, breathing out black smoke. Rustam smiled. He was relieved that no one saw him. Six years of his empty life went sailing off with that ship.

He moved his muscular arms like a demon to surge ahead. Towards the land.

Rustam would no longer be a flotsam.

Translated from the Bengali by Mitali Chakravarty

Mistress of Melodies

1912: Inside a music shop in Chowringhee, Calcutta.

The opening credits roll in without mentioning the film's title. It starts with just the name of the writer, followed by credits for sound, camera, editing, etc. Then slowly, the camera zooms in on an old-time gramophone and when it settles down on a compact frame, the credits start afresh. Now the name of the production company appears on the same visual: Such-n-Such Production Presents…

When these words disappear, a hand enters the frame and sets the record in motion. Immediately an extremely melodious voice is heard singing:

'Mere dard e jigar ki khabar hi nahin…'

After the thumri in Raga Jhinjhoti, recorded in 1905, plays out, the title of the film appears: *Swaron ki Rani.*

The song is heard by a very handsome, manly yet romantic person, around forty-five years old, seated in a Landau, which he is driving. He stops his coach while the song continues and then he locates the shop from which the song is coming.

He enters the shop and enquires about the singer. Just then the song ends with a voice saying: 'My name is Gauhar Jaan.'

The shopkeeper repeats the name: 'She's the famous Gauhar Jaan Kalkattewali, sir.'

'How many of her records are available with you?'

'About twenty, sir.'

'Pack them all up for me, please.'

The man drives away with the twenty records.

Next, we find the man in his luxurious apartment in Calcutta listening to the same song when his friend, Gyan Dutt enters. Gyan is surprised to find that his friend Nimai Sen, a very rich zamindar from Behrampore in North Bengal, is listening to Gauhar Jaan's songs for the first time. Gyan Dutt, it is obvious, is well acquainted with the name.

'Do you like her voice?' Gyan asks.

'She sounds divine! I regret I lost time in getting acquainted with her singing.'

'She is a divine dancer too… And she knows every form of dance. She has sung in twenty languages, and is an expert in ghazals and thumris,' Gyan rattles on. 'Not only that: she sings the songs of our Nobel Laureate, Rabindranath Tagore, too. Above all, her looks are divine.'

'Really?' Nimai Sen draws out two cigarettes from a golden case, offers one to Gyan and takes one for himself. Gyan takes out a matchbox and lights up both their cigarettes. Then, puffing out a mouthful of smoke, he says, 'She is a celebrity. She is the fashion diva of the day. Look at her popularity—she's on the matchbox!' Gyan holds up the imprint of Gauhar Jaan's beautiful face on one side of the matchbox, adding: 'She will soon look out from the back of imported playing cards… Everyone falls in love with her.'

Then they talk about the next day's race at the Maidan and the horses to bet on, particularly the ones owned by Nimai Sen.

II

Next day, Nimai Sen is seen watching the race. Gyan arrives and wants to know the fate of Nimai's horse Shiraz. Nimai informs him that the horse has won. Gyan proposes to take him to the famous Hazarduari Palace in the city of Murshidabad—associated with the name of Sirajuddaula—near Berhampore where Nimai Sen hails from. He is well known in north Bengal as well as in the elite society in Calcutta for his passion for race horses and his dignified and cultured behaviour. So the organizers of the Hazarduari mehfil gladly invite him to the function being hosted by Janaab Kasim Khan, one of the descendants of the Nawab's family.

Nimai Sen attends the mehfil along with Gyan Dutt, who is a music aficionado and a singer too, so he is well known in the music circle of Calcutta. He is also acquainted with Gauhar Jaan—she looks upon Gyan as a good friend.

And Nimai Sen sees Gauhar for the first time when she enters the concert hall and salaams everyone. Her beauty and personality strike Nimai Sen like a flash of lightning. Then she sings her first song, a thumri that goes: '*Kaise kahoon sharam ki baat* (Oh how can I speak out! It's a matter of dear shame…)'

Nimai Sen, who has an artistic soul, is mesmerized. He is transported to a world of divine sensuality, an ecstasy he has never experienced so far. And while she sings and dances, he notices that her eyes are mostly on him. He is thrilled.

And Gauhar Jaan especially notes that Nimai Sen refused

whisky when it was being served to the respectable and rich gathering. She is impressed.

After the first song, Gauhar goes in to rest. When she returns, she is wearing a different dress. She now sings a ghazal, '*Nazar toy hoy gayee jigar ke paar* (O beloved, your glance has pierced me, right through my heart...)'

And as she sings and dances, her eyes meet those of Nimai Sen. Gauhar is bedecked with diamonds and as she turns her face, or pirouettes, the diamonds in her nose-pin dazzle with their brilliance.

As a sign of appreciation, the wealthy listeners shower her with hundred-rupee notes. Nimai Sen tosses five hundred-rupee notes at her. Gauhar salutes with a kurnish and says musically, 'I am indebted to you for your appreciation, janaab!'

She starts singing a different ghazal now: '*Naina se naina miley jaraa...*'

The mehfil ends late at night. When Nimai takes leave and walks towards the exit door, a maid appears and requests Nimai Sen and Gyan Dutt to meet Gauhar Jaan, who desires to pay her compliments.

Nimai Sen meets Gauhar. 'You are exceptional,' he tells her. Her nose pin flashes again as she smiles. 'Thank you very much,' she says with a salaam.

Nimai Sen says, 'I regret discovering you so late!'

She smiles back at him and says, 'Don't regret, sir. Better late than never.'

And they all laugh together.

Gauhar already knows Gyan. She says to Nimai Sen, 'Please set your feet in my Calcutta house. Don't forget...'

'I shall be honoured,' he promises her.

Next morning before leaving for Calcutta, while they are having tea, Gyan briefly narrates Gauhar Jaan Kalkattewali's past to Nimai.

By blood she is an Armenian, a Christian, born in Azamgarh. Her father, William Robert Yeoward, was an engineer who had migrated to India years ago. Gauhar's given name was Eileen Angelina Yeoward. After her father divorced her mother Victoria Hemmings, an Indian by birth, in 1879, Victoria married a Muslim nobleman from Benaras, named Khursheed, and converted to Islam. Eileen Angelina was six years old then. The mother's and daughter's names were changed to Malka Jaan and Gauhar Jaan.

Trained in music and dance, Malka Jaan could sing very well. And Gauhar, since her childhood, showed signs of a musical genius. In time, Malka was recognized as an accomplished singer and became a Kathak dancer in the court of Banaras. She came to be identified as Badi Malka since there were three other courtesans by the name of Malka Jaan—of Agra, of Mulk Pukhraj, and Chulbuli. Badi Malka shifted to Hyderabad and in 1883, when Gauhar was ten years old, her patron, Nizam Asaf Jah VI Mir Mahboob Ali (father of the last Nizam, Mir Osman Ali), brought them back to Calcutta where Nawab Wajid Ali Shah of Oudh had settled. Soon Malka Jaan purchased a house in Chitpore Road where Gauhar trained in Hindustani music under the tutelage of the ustads of Patiala and Rampur gharana; in Dhrupad and in Kathak from Bindadin Maharaj of Lucknow. And in 1886 she gave her maiden performance in the court of Darbhanga.

'Now, after performing at the crowning ceremony of George V in Delhi, she is the topmost professional, a genius in music and dance…' concluded Gyan.

'A genius and a beauty! But what about her life? The men in her life...?' Nimai Sen asks with a smile.

Gyan smiles too. 'She had her affairs, but her first love is music,' he replies. 'Not only that, she is Calcutta's heartthrob. Ladies imitate her hairstyle and dresses. Men buy her photos sold in street corners—'

'Wonderful!' Nimai smiles again.

Back in Calcutta, Nimai Sen cannot forget Gauhar. Her nose pin flashes through his mind as her image repeatedly returns to him. And he recollects her invitation: 'Please set your feet in my Calcutta house—don't forget.'

Finally Gauhar's flashing nose pin makes him set out in his Landau and drive to Gauhar Manzil, a palatial residence at Chitpore Road.

Gauhar Jaan receives Nimai with great warmth and respect. Sen invites her to Berhampore and also to watch his race horses.

Gauhar introduces Nimai to her mother. Malka Jaan is forced to sing a few lines and then recites a few shers that she has composed. Nimai Sen is greatly impressed and touches her feet. That evening Gauhar sings on the terrace of her house for Nimai Sen: '*Saanwariya thahron Jamuna ke teer* (Wait for me, my love, on the banks of Jamuna...)'

While singing, she holds the hands of Nimai Sen, love pulsating through her fingers. He embraces her. She responds.

At that very moment, one of her many records is played in some house: '*Tan man ki sudh bisar gayee... Kaise bajayee bansuriyaa* (I have no sense of body or soul... such is the spell of your flute...)'

In another house four men are sipping whisky while playing

cards. One distributes. On all the cards are pictures of Gauhar Jaan. One man kisses her image and smiles at his partners when a record plays off-frame: '*Tumhari yaad ne mara nazar bhar mein* (I am slayed by the mere recollection of your glance…)'

After some days, Nimai Sen takes Gauhar's leave, for he has to go to Berhampore to solve some problems in his estate. Also, his sixteen-year-old daughter has to be married; some negotiations are on.

'Come back soon, sir,' she says as she stares at him intently.

Nimai Sen has only one child: a daughter. And he has a wife who is very suspicious and extremely possessive about her husband. Her cousin brother who stays in Calcutta regularly informs her about Nimai Sen's races, about his horses, and now about his acquaintance with Gauhar Jaan. 'Nimai drives his Landau through the streets of Calcutta with Gauhar by his side.' Nimai Sen has a confrontation with his wife Maya.

He has tremendous work pressure, and is worried about the economic condition of his estate. He has to pay huge interest for the loans he has taken by mortgaging some landed property or the other.

Then he hears about the proposals for his daughter Charu, a lively and affectionate girl. One sounds good. The boy is a newly appointed ICS officer and also very handsome. He approves of the boy. So does his wife.

But at night she suddenly questions him: 'Do you still love me?'

'What a question!' Nimai smiles. 'You are my wife, Maya!'

'Don't ever forget that,' Maya chews out the words.

And Nimai Sen remembers a face—that of Gauhar Jaan.

Next day he receives a letter from the Maharaja of Kasimbazar. It is an invitation to a 'musical night' that the maharaja has arranged in his palace on the occasion of the Annaprasan, the first rice-eating ceremony, of his first grandson. Celebrated musicians such as Gauhar Jaan Kalkattewali will be singing and dancing. Along with this invitation he receives a letter from Gauhar too, informing him about her visit to Kasimbazar Palace and her hope of meeting him there.

Nimai immediately sends her a letter inviting her to stay in his house as the palace is not very far from Berhampore.

Soon comes the reply that she will stay one evening after she leaves the Maharaja's palace. Nimai Sen is elated at the prospect of meeting Gauhar.

Gauhar wins the hearts of everyone in the maharaja's hall with her songs and dances. She starts with a Turkish song, '*Paad shahem majook yesha.*' Then she sings in English, 'My love is like a little bird…' Next she sings a Bengali song, '*Phaanki diye praner paakhi urey gelo aar elo naa* (The life bird escapes me, and never does it return…)'

And after every song she sings, her eyes settle on Nimai Sen.

The audience is ecstatic. Nimai takes her up to her green room. And, unseen by anybody, a smiling Gauhar stops, comes close to Nimai, holds his hand and whispers, 'I was waiting for this moment, Sen Saheb!'

He goes back to the hall. Gauhar Jaan now shows her skill by dancing on a large sheet of white cloth spread upon another sheet with perfumed red powder sprinkled all over it. A man announces that Bibi Gauhar Jaan will now exhibit her famous 'Lotus Dance'.

The music starts. Gauhar dances exquisitely, with very rapid steps, around the two sheets. Then suddenly she steps upon the white sheet in slow motion. As light as a butterfly she goes around it, with exquisite body movements, expressing with her eyes and various mudras a lotus in bloom.

The audience watches with bated breath. After some time Gauhar steps out of the white sheet and bows to the assembly. Her dance has ended.

Some men come forward, carefully lift the white sheet and delicately spread it out on the floor. Everyone notices with amazement that a perfect lotus has been imprinted on the sheet.

The audience goes wild in appreciation. Gauhar Jaan bows to all.

Then she sings a devotional bhajan: *'Radhey Krishna bol, mukhse Radhey Krishna bol'*... She sings so well that she brings to mind the legendary Meera Bai. People feel the presence of divinity and cry out, '*Hari bol, Hari bol...*'

After two days she takes leave of the maharaja and reaches the pleasure-house of Nimai Sen. It has been specially decorated for her and her troupe of musicians.

Inside, Nimai himself prepares tea for Gauhar. He boils the water by burning hundred-rupee notes. When he serves the tea to her, she exclaims, 'Are you mad, Sen Saheb?'

'Yes. Mad about Gauhar Jaan. A superb artiste. A divine singer. A mesmerizing dancer...'

She is stunned. 'You love me so much?'

He only smiles in reply. They both stare at each other with love in their eyes.

After Gauhar departs, Nimai returns to his building and

has to face Maya's jealous eyes. Nimai feels guilty but strange, he cannot get rid of his growing obsession with Gauhar Jaan.

The other bais of the city all love Gauhar and accept her as the 'Noor' amongst them. Some of them are her friends—especially Agrawali Malka and Jaddanbai, mother of the legendary actress Nargis. From Gauhar's talks, they can sense that she's infatuated with Nimai Sen. Badi Malka hears them talk and walks away silently.

The Bais talk about the national awakening and the anti-British movement. Then they talk about the impending introduction of electricity to Calcutta. They clap with delight, for it sounds like a miracle. Then they talk about the Fancy Fair which is held every year. Organized by the Europeans of the city, it is open to the rajas and the affluent Indians too. They decide to go to the fair the next day.

The governor of Bengal and the police commissioner, both blue-eyed Brits, are walking through the fair with their bodyguards and soldiers trailing them. The fair is looking like a mela of beauties, both European and Indian. Suddenly they notice a royal phaeton drawn by four horses, with a stunningly fair and well-dressed young lady seated therein, being driven leisurely by a coachman with two grooms standing on footboards, all of them well-liveried.

The lady, as her phaeton passes the governor, salaams twice at him. When the phaeton goes forward the governor, who has mistaken her to be a rani or a princess of some state, learns from the police commissioner that she is the celebrated baiji—Bibi Gauhar Jaan Kalkattewali. 'Oh! What a shame,' he mutters to himself.

Next day the governor prohibits the entry of any woman

into the Fancy Fair. When curious people learn the truth, they all have a hearty laugh. The world of baijis has a hearty laugh too as they congratulate Gauhar Jaan.

Soon electricity comes to Calcutta. Gauhar Jaan's 'star' profile has multiplied. The sale of her pictures at street corners has also gone up. Young students now queue up for her photos.

Not only this. One day, five or six well-dressed college youth seek her audience.

The darwan refuses them entry saying, 'She has to go out for the evening drive.'

Just then Gauhar emerges, dressed for her outing. She notices the students. She goes forward and learns that they have come to listen to her songs and will pay her a fee.

Gauhar gravely says, 'I will sing but shall not accept money from you. Please come in and sit.'

They respectfully take their seat. Then Gauhar makes them write down the names of their guardians and their addresses. Thereafter she sings a thumri with the sarangi to accompany her: '*Saanwariya man har lino* (My amour has ensnared my heart…)'

When the song is over the young men thank her. Gauhar says, 'Don't ever go to the house of a baiji as long as you are students. If I come to know, I shall inform your guardians, mind you.'

The students leave her place, sheepishly.

Then she finds Nimai Sen seated at a distance. He had arrived while she was singing and had unobtrusively taken his seat. She runs to him, takes his hand in hers and drags him inside.

They meet Badi Malka Jaan and leave after some pleasantries. Gauhar and Nimai both feel that Badi Malka likes Nimai Sen.

They go to Gauhar's bedroom where Nimai presents her

with a diamond ring. It is a large diamond that seems to be worth at least a lakh.

Nimai Sen wants to leave but Gauhar says, 'I'll show you something. Today you have visited me—that's why electricity also has reached my manzil.' She switches on the lights, shuts the door, comes very close to Nimai, removes her diamond-studded nose pin and whispers, 'Take it, my love! It's yours from tonight.'

Nimai Sen fails to realize the significance of this gesture. 'It's nath-utarna, the removal of the nose pin,' Gauhar explains to him. It is a system practiced by the baijis. A nath is the symbol of their love, their heart—they do not part with it as long as they do not feel inseparable from a particular man.

Gauhar concludes by whispering, 'You are the man for whom I part with my nath. Please take it and be my love, my lord!'

Nimai Sen accepts the nath and becomes her chosen man—her lover and her lord.

Gauhar has purchased a big, modern building in the westernized area of Calcutta—on Free School Street. She frequents it now to supervise the decoration work going on. At times Nimai Sen goes with her in his Landau or sits with her in her royal phaeton.

One day they have to stop as a group of anti-British Congress workers pass through the street, blocking the traffic and raising the slogan of '*Bande Mataram*'.

Gauhar has read Bankim Chandra's novel, *Anandmath*, which has the song '*Bande Mataram*' in it. When the phaeton moves again she starts humming the song, instantly adorning it with classical touches. Gauhar feels that the song is a bridge between Sanskrit and Bengali and needs a touch of classicism that comes from Raag Dhrupad. Nimai appreciates her idea and her sensitivity. And when she tries out the tune, tears roll from her dreamy eyes.

Badi Malka hears this tune and tells Nimai about the silent blessing showered upon Gauhar when she was only eleven by no less a person than the Divine Ramkrishna Paramhans.

Their conversation now settles down on Radha Krishna, for most of the songs Gauhar sings is about the love between these two icons. Nimai Sen explains the significance of the love between Radha and Krishna by giving a spiritual interpretation of their union. Gauhar is fascinated and requests Nimai to get her a good portrait of the duo. Nimai promises to fulfil her wish.

Gauhar now informs him that she will be going on a tour for about a month and invites him to tour with her. But Nimai has no time, as his daughter's marriage has been fixed. A tearful Gauhar regrets that she will miss the wonderful function. She then requests him to take her to the venue where the nationalist poet, Mukunda Das, is to sing the next day. The balladeer, identified by the sobriquet Chaaran Kabi, has turned into a legend by this time as the singer-composer has contributed to the spread of the Swadeshi movement in rural Bengal by inspiring many persons to turn into active nationalists.

'You must go in a disguise, Gauhar. Else people will recognize you and Mukunda Das will be overshadowed and the impact of his inspiring songs will be lost.'

Gauhar agrees and, as suggested by Nimai, dresses as an ordinary housewife and reaches the venue. She covers her head with the pallu of her sari and put sindoor between her brows and in the parting of her hair, and accompanies Nimai Sen as if she is his wife.

She is exceedingly affected by the songs of the wandering minstrel. One of the songs goes thus: '*Bhenge dao reshmi churi aar poro na Banga nari* (O women of Bengal! Wear no more the glittering bangles and the silken sarees…)'

Another says: 'Beware, beware! The sword of justice will not spare you…'

While returning from the programme, Gauhar suggests they stop at a photographer's studio and get photographed in that disguise. Nimai Sen laughs heartily as both sit side by side to pose for the photo.

Badi Malka has been sick. The doctor takes Gauhar aside and cautions her. She appoints three Anglo-Indian nurses to look after her mother round the clock. She also requests friends in the Nizam's Palace in Calcutta to send a reliable man to look after Badi Malka and the house. And before she sets out on her month-long tour, an attractive and well-behaved man of thirty-five, Abbas, is appointed.

While talking sher-o-shayari, Badi Malka quotes some Urdu poets, particularly one Akbar Allahabadi. Gauhar Jaan likes his sher immensely. While touring north India, Gauhar meets Allahabadi in a mehfil and is struck by his personality. He compliments her as an exceptional singer and dancer. She proposes to present him to Calcutta. He declines but offers to send her a sher penned for her.

In the meantime Nimai Sen's daughter is married off with pomp and pageantry. While in Berhampore, Nimai has to face a jealous wife who constantly nags him regarding Gauhar. And suddenly news reaches him that two of his race horses are sick. He hurries back to Calcutta.

Gauhar comes across Agrawali Malka in a mehfil organized by one Singhji in Delhi. There, the two friends sing one after the other and win laurels. But Gauhar misses Nimai Sen.

Nimai Sen's race horses die one after another due to an infection. And misfortune never comes alone: one Nagarmal from whom he had taken a loan of two lakh rupees files a case against him. He feels lonely and remembers Gauhar.

At that very moment, a painter friend arrives. 'You need me urgently, Mr Sen. Why?' Nimai requests him to paint a portrait for him, a portrait of Radha-Krishna.

Gauhar returns to Calcutta and joyously exclaims, 'Oh God! I breathe better in my Calcutta.'

Nimai Sen hears about her return but he is running after legal experts.

Gauhar is saddened by the doctor's report: Badi Malka's condition is serious. She finds the man Abbas very useful, performing well at both the houses, at Chitpore as well as at Free School Street. He has a good sense of décor, and the new house looks marvellous. Above all, the man is so humble.

Nimai Sen goes to the Chitpore house first, meets Badi Malka who treats him very affectionately. Learning that Gauhar is at Free School Street, he reaches that house. He notices Abbas for the first time. When he is introduced to Nimai, Abbas bows respectfully and leaves.

Nimai and Gauhar embrace each other. He then presents her with a copy of their photo taken after visiting Mukunda Das. They look like a married couple. Both laugh.

Nimai then presents her with a set of ivory dolls worth at least a lakh of rupees.

She complains, 'Why do you shower money on me like this?'

Nimai replies, 'I regret it is too little a gift.'

Gauhar urges Nimai to give up racing and stop wasting

money. Nimai does not give out his losses, nor does he agree with Gauhar's logic. He asks her, 'Would you give up your mujras?'

Nimai feels like leaving but Gauhar starts singing a Darbari Tarana and dances to block his path: *'Jao jao jao, mujhse na bolo, sautan ke sang raho.'*

Her song and dance are so captivating that Nimai cannot tear himself away. He has to stay.

The song and the dance lead to a game of love.

And outside the room Abbas waits like a statue, his eyes burning.

The next day a short letter arrives from Akbar Allahabadi. A very formal letter with a short sher:

> *Khushnaseeb zamaney mein kaun hai Gauhar ke siwa?*
> *Sab kuchh Allah ne de rakha hai shauhar ke siwa…*
>
> In this world, who is more fortunate than Gauhar?
> Allah has granted her everything—except a husband…

Badi Malka reads the letter on her bed and nods her head. 'So very true! Now find one, my daughter.'

'What do you think of Nimai Sen, Ammijaan?' Gauhar whispers.

Badi Malka replies, 'He is a true gentleman! *Asli cheez hai…* But will he marry? Find out.'

Badi Malka distracts Gauhar by ordering her to open her almirah and bring out her jewellery box from the safe.

Gauhar does so.

Her mother takes out a locket studded with a big blue diamond. This was gifted to Malka Jaan by the late Nizam, Mir

Mahbub Ali. It is called the Zamrud Heera and is worth five lakh rupees.

'This is my gift to your shauhar, beti!' Malka says.

The next day in his Calcutta house Nimai is looking at the photo of the two of them: himself and Gauhar.

At that moment, in her Free School Street house, Gauhar discovers that Abbas is a gifted tabla player. Nay, a master. She has suddenly arrived, without prior notice.

'Play with me, Abbas, if you can,' Gauhar tells him and starts singing a Khamaj Thumri: '*Kuhu koela kook rahi ban mein* (Kuhu…kuhu…coos the cuckoo in the forest…)'

Abbas plays wonderfully and elicits the best in Gauhar. When the song ends, she gazes fixedly at him.

Abbas stands up and matches her gaze.

Just then Nimai Sen enters saying, 'Are you in, Gauhar?' And he finds Gauhar and Abbas gazing at each other, standing very close.

The spell is broken by his entrance but Nimai has noted it.

Gauhar smiles and praises Abbas to Nimai Sen. 'I have discovered just now that Abbas is an ustad on the tabla…'

'Really? I will hear him one day.'

Abbas politely bows and leaves the room.

Gauhar tells Nimai about Allahabadi's letter and recites the sher.

Nimai says, 'The poet is absolutely right.'

'Is that all? Tell me, how do I get a shauhar?'

Nimai Sen dryly replies, 'First find out if you need one.'

Saying this, he abruptly leaves. Gauhar is saddened and depressed.

That very evening Nimai Sen leaves for Berhampore. A new catastrophe has to be tackled. A fresh case has been filed against him by a man who had given him a loan.

And the very next day Badi Malka dies.

Every single baiji of Calcutta, Jaddan Bai, Munni Bai and Malka Agrawali included, and all the patrons of Gauhar crowd the Chitpore house.

Gauhar cannot live in that house any more. She starts living mostly in the Free School Street house.

One day she runs into Gyan Dutt. She enquires about Nimai Sen. But Gyan cannot help her since he has given his word to Nimai that he will not divulge his whereabouts.

That afternoon she goes out alone in her phaeton. She drives for long. She returns in the evening, takes out a bottle of whisky, pours a drink and calls Abbas. She orders him to play the tabla. She starts dancing. She gets drunk while dancing and commands Abbas to also drink and play. Ultimately she surrenders to an emboldened Abbas.

Nimai Sen loses every court case against him. But somehow he saves the family house in Berhampore. Then he takes leave of a weeping wife.

The baijis have come to know of Gauhar's affair with Abbas. They regret this, for they all like Nimai Sen and hold him in great regard. Jaddan tries to contact Gauhar and requests her to stop her liaison with Abbas but Gauhar pays no heed.

Abbas lovingly offers drinks to Gauhar and makes her sign letters. She signs them in her drunken state while Abbas plays on the tabla. But when she is alone she sometimes sits staring at the photo with Nimai Sen.

One day, Abbas asks her, 'When are you going to marry me, Bibijaan? I refuse to remain a bharwa—I want to be your shauhar.'

Gauhar is shocked. Then, within days she realizes that Abbas is a crook, an exploiter who has appropriated the houses at Chitpore as well as Free School Street by making her sign papers in a drunken state. She returns to her senses, goes to O.C. Ganguly, the top-most attorney, and files a case against Abbas. She sells her ornaments and this becomes her obsession: she *must* win the cases against Abbas.

Fate is cruel to Nimai Sen. He has lost everything. He has left Berhampore. He has been offered loving shelter by the Maharaja of Kasimbazar, a friend. And he is sick. He is sick at heart and has a broken heart too.

But is fate kind to Gauhar who had everything in the world, save a shauhar? No. She too has lost everything. She has lost 'love' and that is more precious than a shauhar. She had taken huge loans to pay the lawyers. She had mortgaged the houses too. Now she has won the legal battle but cannot pay the money-lenders, for she has bid goodbye to her profession too during this period. Agrawali Malka weeps as she lovingly shelters Gauhar in her house.

Suddenly Gyan Dutt comes to meet her one day. He informs her that Nimai Sen is on his deathbed and wants to see Gauhar and hear her sing one last time. She runs to her room, takes out the Zamrud diamond that her Ammijaan had given for her shauhar, and then accompanies Gyan to Satyen Pal's house.

But she is late. Nimai Sen is dead when she stands before him, after two years.

Satyen Pal says, 'He has left two things for you: a painting of Radha Krishna, and this diamond nose pin.'

He hands them over to Gauhar. She looks at the painting. Radha and Krishna are beaming at her.

'He very much wanted to hear you sing before he breathed his last. But he died quietly, peacefully,' Satyen Pal tells her.

Gauhar Jaan falls at the feet of Nimai Sen and stays still. Then she lifts up her head, looks at the painting and starts to sing:

Radhey Krishna bol, mukhsey Radhey Krishna bol…
Maaya se man lubhaya
Is maaya ne gher liya.
O dukhan ke palla chhor
Mukhse Radhey Krishna bol…

And tears stream down her cheeks.

It is the last chapter of Gauhar's life.

Jaddan, Agrawali Malka, Munni Bai and many other musicians are worried about Gauhar who no longer goes out for mujras. They are concerned. Finally Jaddan arranges a job for Gauhar. She shall become the court singer of Raja Krishna Wodeyar IV of Mysore.

Gauhar agrees.

There, in the court of Mysore, she sings her first song for the Maharaja: '*Piya bina aawat naahi chain* (Peace there is no more, since my love is gone.)'

One day she feels a flutter in her heart and fails to attend the court.

The maharaja visits her. She says, 'My time has come, O Maharaja. Please do one thing for me.'

'What is it, Gauhar Jaanji?'

Gauhar brings out the Zamrud diamond and her nose pin and says, 'Please offer them to the Dancing Shiva in your court. Please.'

Without a word, the maharaja accepts them and leaves her.

In the evening, in her room, Gauhar looks at the photo of herself and Nimai Sen, then at the painting of Radha Krishna, plucks the strings of the tanpura and starts to sing, '*Ekhane man basey naa…*'

While singing, the tanpura slips from her hands. Her song stops. She clutches her heart and falls. But the song goes on—'*Ekhane man basey naa…*'

This is the first draft of a screenplay that the author had planned. He wrote it in English—as he used to write all his scripts.

ALSO IN SPEAKING TIGER

That Bird Called Happiness: Stories

NABENDU GHOSH

EDITED BY RATNOTTAMA SENGUPTA

FOREWORD BY GULZAR

'The stories in this collection are evocative of the films Nabendu Ghosh scripted—bold, nuanced, meaningful—a writer's films. The humanism of *Sujata* and *Bandini*, the overweening need for love despite its demands in *Abhimaan*, the emotional core of *Parineeta*—these are evident as tonal strands and thematic concerns of the collection.' —Kitaab.org

In this collection—ranging from stories of love found and lost to tales of the supernatural—Ghosh masterfully traces the inscrutable ways of the human heart. The reigning queen of Bombay cinema allows a younger leading man to fall in love with her to spite her husband. A schoolmaster's ravishing wife joins him in the small town where he works, inspires him to build a garden for her, and sets about wrecking his life. An impoverished student sits across a purdah from a nawab's begum; she dictates letters to her husband and, as the student takes down her words, he falls into forbidden love with the voice from across the screen. And an unbending priest from Noakhali finds all the principles of his life upended after Muslim rioters kidnap his daughter.

Marked by psychological insight, keen observation and vivid prose, *That Bird Called Happiness* brings to readers the work of one of the greats—not only of Bengali literature but of the Indian literary canon.